A PLACE

A true story of the life
of a boy from

B. A. Hyde-Tingley

With Best Wishes

Bernard A Hyde-Tingley

1990

ARTHUR H. STOCKWELL LTD.
Elms Court Ilfracombe
Devon

ISBN 0 7223 2398-0
Printed in Great Britain by
Arthur H. Stockwell Ltd.
Elms Court Ilfracombe
Devon

To the memory of my father and mother
Thomas Arthur and Elsie Amelea Hyde-Tingley

ACKNOWLEDGMENTS

I wish to express my deepest thanks to my cousin, Carol N. Coates, for checking my information relating to Northleach, and its peoples; also to Lional and Linda Kay, Roy and Rosalind Tingley and Miss M. Baxendale for sharing the typing of the manuscript; and to my family for their support and encouragement in its preparation.

I would also like to express my sincere thanks to Arthur H. Stockwell Ltd. (publisher) who have been most helpful and understanding in the publication of this book.

Illustrations set between pp. 32-37

CHAPTERS

CHAPTER 1

Traveller's Return

As I stood on the brow of Clack Hill, just below the village of Bradenstoke-come-Clack, overlooking the Vale of Dauntsey, I could just see the roofs of the train on which I had travelled still standing at the platform of Dauntsey station; apparently in no hurry to proceed on its way to the westerly towns of, Chippenham, Bath and Bristol. I had arrived at Dauntsey from Swindon, on the fourteenth day of August 1945, exactly four years to the day since I had bidden farewell to my family and walked down the same hill to catch my connection which would return me to my unit at Bradford on Avon, from where I expected to move to my embarkation port at Avonmouth.

It was with a feeling of awe that I became conscious that I was witnessing what to me was nothing short of a miracle, since I, unlike so many of my comrades, had been spared and allowed to return to my loved ones. At that moment I stood and gazed around me at a patchwork of countryside, a little part of my England, my homeland, a place I would eventually explore and get to know and love, and all its people. Looking around I could see the rays of the setting sun shining through the ash trees in the fields, bringing beautiful shades of colour to the hedgerows, from which I could detect a faint aroma of the various flowers and vegetation. The significance of the beauty which greeted me, was enhanced by the numerous bird-songs, which I had begun to recognise after a long absence.

Turning to resume my climb up the hill to the village, I noticed a lone blackbird on one of the ash trees nearby. It was rendering its last lullaby of the evening which to me was the most beautiful welcome and vesper all rolled into one. My heart was indeed full as I slowly resumed my walk to the village hardly realising that I was actually home in this beloved country of mine and that I would shortly be meeting my loved ones again.

The village itself rests along the top of chalk hills overlooking some of the most beautiful countryside which stretches as far as the eye can see towards the Bristol Channel. There is just the one road through the village starting at Lyneham, then travelling for a mile or so through a hedge-lined lane, it enters the village and continues onto the hill I was ascending. The nearest public transport was at the bottom of the hill at Dauntsey Lock, where both trains and local buses could be found fairly regularly. I found that the village possessed a fine old church, a Methodist Church and a Baptist Chapel. There was a typical village shop, with its post office and its own bakery. There was a wealth of period cottages, and in the fields to the west were the remains of the old Abbey, known as Clack Abbey. On a fine day one could see, faintly in the distance, a sister Abbey in the town of Malmesbury some seven miles away across the vale.

My family moved to the village in 1940 while I was in France and I had little chance to explore the village and surrounding countryside. However, I had been able to take with me on my departure, memories of the friendly villagers who had accepted my family and had shown great kindness over the following years. The reason for my family moving to Bradenstoke from the Cotswold town of Northleach was that father had been engaged to organise catering facilities for the work-force who were building the local aerodrome, and double summer-time found hundreds of men working almost non-stop round the clock, on buildings and runways.

Apparently, all my family became involved in the war effort at one time or another, mainly in catering. Sister Pat was on assembly of gliders, and met Amy Johnson several times. Amy's job was to ferry to other aerodromes. I understand the enemy left their calling cards several times and brought a sense of urgency to the work-force, and more than a little sadness to some of the local homes.

My brother Douglas had soon made friends with the lads of the village but he has his own stories to tell of the war years in Bradenstoke. At the age of fourteen, he experienced the crash of a fighter plane a few hundred yards from the house. The plane finished up in the hedge and burst into flames. My brother had run to help out and found the young pilot trapped in the cockpit. He was desperately trying to free himself but apparently his legs were held too firmly. The fire tender arrived but no one could get anywhere near to help. The cries of the pilot were soon lost in the raging inferno. The sights and sounds were to remain in my brother's mind for many years. I was to hear many such stories in the following years.

My thoughts as I continued my unhurried stroll up to the village were interrupted by the voice of an elderly gentleman who bade me good evening, as he walked with his dog, which I greeted with a pat. And a good evening it was indeed! I had been lost in thought, breathing in deeply of the beauty that surrounded me, wondering what the future held for us all and how I would react to living at peace once again. A freedom and peace bought dearly by the lives of so many of my service pals. Men who were now resting in graves scattered over many parts; in the fields of France and in desert wastes, not one forgotten but held in one's heart in fond memory and great respect after the years we had served together.

By now I had come within sight of the village and from the evening dusk I heard the sound of women in conversation. As I drew nearer to them a voice came to me asking.

"Is that you Bern?" It was the voice of my dear mother and at that moment I was reminded of another occasion when from the gloom mother called to me, "Is that you Bern?"

For a moment of time the world stood still as I remembered a time and place many years before and in very different circumstances. As you will see, it all began in the Cotswolds.

CHAPTER 2

The Cotswold Lad

I was born in the market town of Northleach in Gloucestershire, on December 11th 1919. At the beginning of 1920 my father and mother were able to purchase the rather prominent premises standing at the west corner of the market-place. This property was to be known as "The Cotswold Stores", and became the family home for my mother, father and six children. I had four sisters and a brother, the last to arrive. The Cotswold Stores soon became a household name and thanks to my parents' ability, the business grew into a first-class provision and grocery store, having separate departments for ladies, gents and children's outfitting.

Father had a good knowledge of business and brought many new ideas from his home town of Brighton, and with mother's ability as bookkeeper, having had many years experience with a firm in Cirencester, the stores prospered. Our staff were local people. Several lads were engaged from the local workhouse and proved to be the most willing workers in the garden and around the shop. They were also keen to work with the livestock since father bred his own pigs and poultry, killing and curing bacon in the bacon warehouse at the rear of the shop.

Home produced bacon, cooked hams, brawn and pies, were in great demand. It was a six-day week for my mother and father, which meant that it was necessary to employ a woman to care for the household demands. We had a nurse for the children and visiting governess to teach us older children. The nursemaid would get us washed and dressed each morning ready for when the governess arrived to teach us from 10.00 a.m. till 12 noon. In the afternoons, in nice weather, she would drive us out into the country lanes in the family pony and trap.

We would sometimes stop near a field covered in buttercups and daisies. We would be shown how to make daisy-chains and would decorate the heads of my sisters. We were awfully sad when one day our friend did not turn up for our lessons and a little while afterwards we were told that she was in hospital, and later had moved away. We were then taught privately by the wife of a business man who had the petrol station and shop opposite. She had taught prior to her marriage and proved most keen and helpful to us and kept us interested from 10.00 a.m. till 12 noon. Afternoons were spent in the company of our nanny who would take us for walks when the weather allowed. Sometimes we were allowed to visit the show grounds on Carnival day.

In the July of 1923, my father and mother had their own stall of sweets, fruits and soft drinks. It was in this year that my father's relations came from Brighton to join in the festivities. It was also the first time that he produced ice-cream, using the recipe he had collected from Italy where he had served in the war. I was a spoilt child and expected the first penny cornet. As I walked amongst the crowds children saw me and there was a rush for the ice-cream. This was indeed a treat to come to Northleach. The roundabouts belonging to the family firm of Nicholls, caused much excitement with their galloping horses and coloured bunting. We were too young to be allowed to ride on them.

The Northleach mop was held in the market-place in view of our home. We could watch the arrival of the steam wagons pulling the trailers which transported the swings and roundabouts. After a few hours of hard work, the fair was erected and stood festooned with coloured bunting, lights and brightly coloured and painted woodwork. Many stalls stood around the square selling all sorts of goods, paper hats, toys, sweets, popcorn, toffee-apples, and we were allowed to watch one stall holder making coloured rock and toffee. The brown and white rock twists were made by his wife. She would collect a large block of sticky mass from the pan in which it had boiled, and then stretching it in her hands she would begin to pull it into a long roll. This she would loop over a large hook on the side of the stall and would pull hard until the soft rock stretched quite a lot. She would then twist it. This process continued until the whole rock was striped brown and white and looked lovely. However, we did not fancy eating it because we had noticed that the woman would spit on her hands from time to time. After a time for setting, the sweet was cut into lengths or chopped into pieces.

The stalls were piled up with coloured sliced coconut, rock and peanuts. Other stalls sold baked potatoes and hot chestnuts. There were coconut shies, an Aunt Sally and darts. So it was most exciting for us to be taken round by our nanny who at times allowed us to purchase a small toy, or a packet of tiger nuts or licorice roots.

Another event of the year, in the twenties, was Guy Fawkes' night, November 5th. It was with interest we would watch the boys and girls of the town collecting waste paper, boxes and rubbish from the shops; while others would go out into the byeways collecting branches from the woods and motor tyres from the only garage. It took at least two days to build the fire to a reasonable height and on the morning of the 5th the prepared fire could be seen in the middle of the market-place awaiting the appointed time for it to be set on fire.

In the afternoon someone would carry a ladder out so that a lad could climb up to erect a guy on the top. This was usually supplied by a kindly parent who would later join in the fun. Someone else would supply treacle toffee and baked potatoes. Everyone awaited the rocket that would be lit and rise up over the town. This was the signal to light the fire. How exciting it was to see the flames rise up and surround the guy. The bright flames lighting up the children's faces as they stood around in a huge circle.

As children we were allowed to have our fireworks in the back garden. These were usually attended to by the shop staff who also made a small fire for us. We watched from the nursery window, hoping that one day when we were older, we would be allowed to make our own fire, light our own sparklers and bake chestnuts and potatoes.

By the age of seven life had become quite interesting for me. There was so much to see and enjoy. I was allowed to walk as far as Granny Hyde's; she was my mother's mother and lived just up the road from the Square. Granny and Grandad Hyde were great chapel folk and proved a great encouragement to us children. It was at this time that our private teacher died and my two eldest sisters and I were found places at the little church school where we soon made friends and were allowed to join in games after school such as marbles, whip and tops, hoops, and hide-and-seek.

I always looked forward to my time at home during the weekends. Sometimes I was allowed to help at the rear of the shop. I felt quite a man at eight years of age weighing up sugar, dried fruit, rice, dried peas and beans; each product had its own coloured bag. The butter and margarine came in huge blocks which had to be cut into smaller blocks of one pound and half pound pats. Each pat was wrapped in a greaseproof paper with a name, "Cotswold Stores". All I did, was under the watchful eye of father who would come and check the various weights. He was a good teacher though sharp at times, and all mistakes had to be corrected in his presence.

It was all hustle and bustle when the Wholesalers, Grimley Hughes of Oxford, delivered their weekly consignments of groceries in the steam wagon. They would park just at the front of the shop and after unloading, the driver would rake the ashes from the fire-box underneath the front of the wagon before departing for his next call.

Our staff worked hard from 8.00 a.m. until 7.00 p.m. except on Saturdays when the shop would remain open until 9.00 p.m. There was so much packing and dispatching of grocery to farms and villages outside the town. Most of the large country houses relied on the Cotswold Stores and my father's name became a household name and was well known for his service to the community. After the shop closed at night, my mother retired to the office to complete the days bookkeeping. Our two delivery men would return the horses to the stable where they were curry combed, fed and watered.

One morning a week was for slaughtering. Pigs were brought in from the fields and when the slaughter man had done his job the carcasses were burnt on a bed of straw to singe all the hairs off, then they were scrubbed well before being taken into the salting and curing house. Here they were hung up and the blood was collected for the making of black puddings. There was nothing wasted everything was used for the consumer. Home-made lard, bath chaps, faggots, chitterling were made, and strangely enough I acquired a liking for all these tasty foods.

Through the darker evenings one of the men would fill and light paraffin lamps, which we hung at various points in the house and yards. In the shop itself there were gas lamps hung in the windows and over the counters. Electricity eventually came to the town, the local brewery having closed, was used to house the huge generator and it was not long before there were street lights, lighting up many of the dark corners and lanes leading from the Square. Many of the large houses and shops received this wonderful service with no need to have smelly lamps in the house, although the lamps had given a sense of warmth but never warm enough to keep the windows free from ice. I often saw children breathing onto the window to clear the ice so that they could see what A. Tingley and Son had to offer for Christmas. The kids with runny noses and rosy cheeks would have a look of excitement and expectation of what Father Christmas may bring them.

The windows were colourful and a pleasing sight especially to the young ones. By the second week of December, Christmas goods had arrived and our windows exploited the Christmas fare to good effect. There were some whole gammons hung up amongst the holly and mistletoe, piles of oranges marked up thirteen to the dozen at one shilling, there were boxes of dates, figs, raisons and nuts of all sorts,

Christmas crackers, puddings and iced cakes. Fancy goods of all sorts on show in the household window were especially of interest to parents. Men from the villages would come in to be measured for a suit while women would order their groceries with a few fancy goods to enhance the Christmas table. I remember at one time when tinned salmon came on to the market, made by John West, the best red salmon at seven pence halfpenny per eight ounce tin; a large tin was less than a shilling at eleven pence halfpenny. Whole gammons were around five shillings each and most regulars had one on their order plus a dozen oranges to which father would add a bag of sugar cubes so that the children could place a cube in a hole they had made in the orange then they would suck the juice through the sugar.

Sometimes on a Saturday morning my father would give me a piece of paper and a pencil so that I could go round the two other grocery shops and check on their prices of bacon etc. On my return he would drop his prices a penny in competition.

Of course, looking back to those days I realise that my father had the advantage in producing much of our own produce. On Friday evenings I would carry a basket of groceries up to Granny Hyde's — no charge — I often wondered why my father was so generous to people, especially to my grandmother and grandfather, despite the fact that sometimes as a child I wondered why few of the relatives would speak to him. In later years I began to find the answers to some of my inner most thoughts. Why did they dislike him so, was it jealousy?

Christmas Eve eventually came bringing the hustle and bustle of last minute shopping. The children still came to watch through the window into the warm atmosphere of the shop. Customers coming and going burdened with Christmas fare. At the most some of these little urchins would find an orange, a sugar mouse and a new penny in their stocking on Christmas morning.

All the other little shops were busy also and my sisters and I had gone round breathing on the windows like the other boys and girls. We too were enjoying the thrills of expectancy. Only when we were called in for our cups of Ovaltine as good "Ovaltinies" and put to bed we knew that Father Christmas would indeed come, little realising that in the not too distant future we too would be in the same situation as the little urchins in the street, when even an orange would be conspicuous by its absence.

Christmas Eve at the shop came to a close, blinds were drawn, the counters covered with sheets, the delivery carts were back, the horses stabled and when all the last jobs were finished all the staff would come into the kitchen, a large room with its iron range aglow, and decorated with holly and ivy. From the walls hung sides of bacon together with a brace of pheasants, a couple of hares and a cockerel all sent in by appreciative farmers. I remember one large Christmas pudding hung from a beam, since it was always customary to keep one for father's birthday in February. Before leaving the staff would receive a glass of ginger wine and mince pies and leave clutching a golden guinea, although the average wage, I believe, was twelve and six pence for an adult male, and ten shillings for a woman.

Sometimes the 'mummers' would call. This was really exciting; they would be invited into the sitting-room, seven of them in number and the whole family would gather around to watch the men with blackened faces and ragged clothes do their charade. One man supposedly drunk, would fall to the floor and one professing to be a witch-doctor would prance around him swinging a balloon on a stick, striking the sick man and chanting a Cotswold rhyme or incantation which did nothing for the poor fellow on the floor. The balloon was usually the bladder from a pig obtained from a butcher. I believe this one had come from our establishment because at the end of the play and after receiving a drink of sherry and a few shillings for charity, one man put his finger to his cap and said, "Thanks for the bladder, gov'nor. Happy Christmas all".

Carol singers also called and sang *Once in Royal David's City*, with music from a little harmonium and light from lanterns on poles. I think the sound of the carol sung in such harmony, will remain with me through life.

CHAPTER 3

Church Bells

In the year 1928 I was nine years old, and so many things stand out in my memory of those days. Being older than my sisters I was allowed to stay with Granny and Grandpa Hyde. Apparently, I had become too much of a handful for the nanny, being utterly spoilt and awfully cheeky, yet I cannot remember ever being punished for my naughtiness. Anyway, it was felt that my grandparents might help me to be a better child. It was the easy way out for my father who should have given me a good smacking. As it was, moving me to my grandmother's, did little to bring my father and me closer together, whereas a good hiding may have made me respect him more. Of course, as I grew older and time passed I understood him better.

My sisters spent most of their time, when not at school, in the company of a maid. So it was that I spent almost a separate life with my grandparents and Cousin Harold who was a few years older than I. My two eldest sisters and I did fairly well at school and had great respect for the headmaster who believed in the rule of the cane. He never caned me because like most of the boys, I absolutely feared the man.

I remember a small brother of one of our maids left the playground to watch the local hounds go by. Unfortunately, he did not hear the bell and only just made his seat in time, but the head had seen him from the window. He must have disliked young Jimmy, for Jimmy was called in and caned across the backs of both hands, which caused much bruising and bleeding. During playtime Jimmy went to his sister and told her what had happened, she in turn took Jimmy to my father who did not hesitate to go to the school and accost the headmaster and told him in no uncertain terms that caning was for the bottoms not the backs of hands. There was less caning afterwards which proved to me that the biggest of men can be cowards at heart.

Sometimes on Saturday mornings I would assist my grandmother in the kitchen, often cleaning knives and forks with brick dust on a knife board. There was always a job of folding newspaper into spills with which to light the fire.

Grandmother always had her daily milk delivered by my Uncle Bob who kept a few cows on his smallholding which was a short walk from the market-place, up what we called the Doctor's Lane because the doctor's surgery was on the corner facing the main street. After hearing from my granny how helpful I had been, Uncle Bob was pleased and asked if I would like to do a job for him one Saturday. Of course I was thrilled and felt quite grown-up.

I said I would ask my parents first. This I did, and the following Saturday morning I presented myself at Uncle Bob's holding; I had a bag in which I carried some sandwiches and a small bottle of lemonade. I also had a walking-stick which I had borrowed from Grandad Hyde. Uncle Bob explained that he wanted me to take his cows for grazing in one of the lanes just outside the town. There were five cows and I would simply walk ahead and lead them through the town, past my school and on until we reached a lane with extra wide verges. I had visions of cows running amok in the town and I wondered what my parents would think if they happened to glance out of the shop window. With tongue in cheek I set off and to my surprise and delight there was a string of five cows lead by a little Jersey cow called Bell, (she had a bell around her neck) which was accepted as the leader. The animals followed at a casual pace and eventually we arrived at the place where uncle had said the cows would start to graze and that I was not to worry as they would all stay within a short distance of Bell.

I was asked to bring the cows back at 3.00 p.m. ready for milking. I said I had no watch but uncle said just listen for the church clock to strike three; and sure enough I could hear the clock quite clearly, even though it must have been a mile away. When I heard the strike of twelve I sat and ate my sandwiches with great relish in the open air. Every three hours the chimes would play the tune of, *O Worship the King All Glorious Above* and I remember laying in the grass listening to the bells that were to mean so much to me in the time to come.

I have heard them ringing for weddings and on Saints Days. I remember them on frosty and misty evenings, at Christmas time, through thick fog in November and on evenings on a bright starry night; sometimes in the early hours of the morning. These bells meant so much to me and I knew I would never lose my way as long as I could hear the bells.

Three o'clock came and sure enough I heard it plainly, it was time to return. I was rather loath to leave this lovely grass verge with its sweet-smelling clover and sainfoin. It had been really satisfying to lay in the long grass listening to the different sounds of the birds. I was gradually getting to know each bird by its sound, and I had begun to learn about nature and was most keen to learn more.

I went forward and gently led my charges toward the town in order to have them home in time for milking. I really did feel my responsibility as we moved in line one behind the other through the streets of the Mill End and then the market-place and on to the smallholding. The result of our journey, nature being what it was, my charges had left their mark in the roads. I suppose there were a few who saw this as something for their gardens.

Those early summer days were a joy to me. I spent many happy hours with my grandfather, who was a watch and clock repairer and also well known as a taxidermist. There were many homes throughout Gloucestershire proudly displaying glass cases of stuffed birds, animals and fish. Some had their favourite pet such as a canary, cat or dog all preserved and presented by my grandfather, Robert Hyde. Grandfather was also a keen huntsman and when too old for riding would catch hold of my hand and say, "Come on Bernie let's follow the hounds!" We would set out with a packet of sandwiches for lunch and then off we would go to watch the meet. Sometimes they would start off down the main street and into the prison copse, a small wood adjacent to the old prison and bordering the road to the village of Hampnett. Perhaps, they would travel through the Mill End and up the school road and past where I had grazed the cows.

There was a wide expanse of fairly level farm land all around here and when the hounds found scent, at Winter Well, a small spinney with farm buildings on the left, they set off at a good pace making for the open country bordering the Chrickley Barrow road, they seemed to fade into the distance and my grandfather turned to me and said, "Well that's it for today Bernie." We turned to leave for home but from the distance we heard the faint call of the horn and then gradually a horse and its rider with scarlet jacket was seen moving from a wood several fields away. Soon this rider was joined by others then we could see the hounds in full cry making back towards us and to our surprise a fox went past in the field near us and soon the panting pack, all mud splattered and frothing at the mouth, went past us following the scent to the next farm of Cats Abbey which lay at the side of a wonderful green lane bordering the town. At this point we decided to return home. I would then leave my grandfather and grandmother to have their afternoon rest and I would go on home to see my mother and father and find out what my sisters had been up to.

Our walks were always most interesting since my grandfather had many stories to tell, usually I believe, with a lesson to be learnt. He was a Sunday school teacher and superintendant. A deeply religious man, who was most lovable. It was such a loss to me when he passed away and I turned my attention more than ever to my grandmother. She too was like my grandfather in her religious convictions and gave me much inspiration in the Christian way of life. I was proud to hold her hand and walk up the chapel aisle to the pew at the front, and in years to follow I was to enjoy such wonderful fellowship here with other young people in Sunday school. Sometimes the whole family would be there for the anniversary or chapel outings by a charabanc to Weston-super-Mare where we were all able to walk along the sands and back to the hall of the Salvation Army for tea. What an exciting day and it was the topic of conversation for many days to follow.

My grandparents had adopted a child, a lad with whom I was to become great pals. He was some years older than I. His name was Harold and a wonderful lad, good living, keen on his adopted parents, such a wonderful example to a boy my age, being about nine years my senior. I found him most wise, yet young enough to share in my boyish games, but old enough to feel responsible for my welfare. He was a joy to be with.

His first job on leaving school was to look after the chickens of our local doctor as well as other jobs including, cleaning the doctor's Model T Ford. Harold took a great interest in the car and this interest was soon to be extended to a motor bike. He had seen one for sale "second hand" and on his sixteenth birthday he had saved up the thirty shillings to buy it. It was called "She" since Harold was heard to say that "She runs well". She was to prove this because it was not long before Harold, with jacket flapping behind him, raced down through the market-place, into the area known as The Green and back up to granny's, most likely breaking the sound barrier at ten miles an hour and with little puffs of bluish smoke following him.

I was proud to be asked to help clean the bike and was thrilled when Harold suggested that I climb on the back and within a few minutes we were out in the lanes. She went well. She was actually a two and a quarter horsepower Norton with a flywheel at the side of the engine. It was necessary to do a push start after priming the engine on an oil pump attached to the petrol tank and once running to Harold's satisfaction we would once again make for the lane near the church. This lane was called the "all alone" and it was beautiful, with a bluebell wood on the right and lovely hedgerow on the left.

One of Harold's hobbies in those days was keeping tame rabbits and it was in this lane that we would forage for cow parsley and dandelions for them. To transport the fodder home it was necessary to build a truck large enough to hold several sacks, out of Tate & Lyle sugar boxes and bicycle wheels. Sometimes I was allowed to ride in the truck, then after filling it I would help pull it home and then feed the rabbits which were Chinchillas and Blue Bevrans — such wonderful creatures.

My Uncle Robert and Aunty Nell had one son called Bobby who was older than us and left Northleach to work away, so we saw little of him. His sister, my cousin Carol, was a great friend of ours. My sisters were thrilled when Carol said she would come and play with them at granny's. Carol worked in a fruit and grocery shop and after work she would bring many of her dolls which my sisters were allowed to help wash and dress. I remember the dolls as having china heads and rag bodies, although one or two were made of celluloid and all were dressed in knitted clothes made by Carol and her mum, Aunty Nell. On an evening such as this I had little time for such things as dolls, so I was allowed to borrow a set of meccano from Harold with which I could build such things as windmills and other working models.

Of course, sometimes my granny had paying guests and our room was needed, so we went home to the shop and my mum and dad. These paying guests were theatrical folk who came to the Town Hall to put on plays. One was an entertainment company and did Shakespearian plays, but normally it was pantomime. I remember one lady and gentleman who came for the weekend and I was fascinated with all their gaudy trimmings and make-up. Late one evening, I was playing in the living room at granny's. I was playing with some foreign coins which my father had given me. He had brought them from abroad and the lady said she would like to borrow the money to use on the stage. She also borrowed some of granny's embroidered cushions from the settee to use as padding under her skirt since she was playing the part of a fat lady. Well, we never did see the return of my money nor the cushions. The name of the show people held a stigma for many years and my granny said that only those too lazy to work would consider taking up acting or perhaps they had not sufficient brains to do a respectable job. Dear old Granny Hyde preached against anything she considered worldly or unchristian.

It was seeing Harold on his motor bike that my father decided he should have one so that he could visit our chicken farm at Lower Guitting, so he purchased a small two and a quarter horsepower

B.S.A. and on Thursday afternoons when the shop was closed he would ask me to ride with him. I had seen him drive before, so it was with some trepidation that I climbed aboard and clung like mad to his back and hung on for dear life. We travelled at fearsome speeds of twenty miles per hour amidst intermittent bangs and puffs of blue smoke. We would pass people in their horse and traps while people in their gardens would look up to see what noisy intruder had the cheek to travel at such speed through their village. We would sometimes visit a farm in the village of Hazelton, a few miles out of Northleach. Here we were allowed to roam along the side of the little stream that meandered through the valley. Dad would sometimes take his four-ten shot-gun and we would shoot grass snakes basking in the sun on the stream bank. I used to take a cap pistol and pretend to do my own shooting.

Some summer evenings I was allowed to help Aunty Nell by delivering some home-made butter to one or two houses, having first helped by turning the handle of the separating machine and watched my auntie turn the butter machine. I was amazed at how long she turned the machine before eventually a beautiful pat of golden butter was produced. This she turned out, weighed and patted into shape and eventually laid in the bottom of a wicker basket in grease-proof paper and I would then start my delivery. Once, after delivering one evening, my aunty offered to pay me a half penny but I pressumed I intended to be a business man one day like my dad, so I asked her to keep it until it grew into a penny. I was reminded of this later in life.

I felt amply repaid when Uncle Bob asked me if I would like to see an aeroplane. Of course I jumped at the chance to see a real plane, apparently Sir Alan Cobham was coming to give joy-rides from a field just outside town.

We made our way to the spot taking a bag of peppermints to moisten our mouths as we watched the little biplane come in to land, taxying down the field, to return and stop within a few yards from where we were; it was not long before the first local chap was encouraged with a gentle push to step forward for the first ride.

The pilot adjusted the straps to hold the fellow in, who sat well down with his peak cap, back to front, and holding on for dear life; then Sir Alan nimbly climbed into his seat and the engine burst into life. With puffs of smoke coming from the exhausts it turned into the wind and was away bouncing down the field. It rose and turned to come roaring over our heads and with a swaying motion it rose higher and higher then it did a complete loop the loop. Then except for the sound of the wind in its strutts (according to the locals standing nearby), it landed and returned to allow the first joy-rider to dismount. Well it was a very wobbly attempt to reach the ground, even to a kid of my age I could see that his face had gone all white and peculiar; poor chap, and it had cost all of two shillings and sixpence.

I was still watching the chap being congratulated by some of his friends when I realised that my uncle had left my side and was about to climb into the plane; he had hardly sat when someone clambered up to take a photograph of him which was later framed and hung in a prominent position in the living-room.

To my pleasant surprise my uncle enjoyed it very much and had he had another two shillings and sixpence I felt sure that he would have gone up again; but in those days that was a day's pay for a man, so there were few there that could afford more than one ride.

It had been quite exciting to me to be allowed to walk up close and actually touch the rear wing, but it was my introduction to a real plane.

It was not long after this that I was at play in the school playground when the airship R 101 passed over, and in later years I heard that it had crashed in France, but it was wonderful to see the huge silver machine sailing along in the sunshine.

It was not until the year of 1937 that I saw my next air machine. It was late one evening when we became aware of engines of some large machine in the sky above Northleach and travelling from the west; as it got nearer we were aware of a searchlight coming from the object and shining on the road; the light took in the whole street including our house, and then it proceeded on towards London. The following day the papers reported that the German Graf Zeppelin had been over on supposedly a friendly visit. I think we all had our own thoughts on that; but I remember how ghostly the awful thing sounded as it travelled what seemed to be just above the roof-tops. It seemed so foreboding, especially to a lad of my age.

CHAPTER 4

The Trauma of Loss

There was little traffic on the streets in those days, there were the odd steam wagons and horse and carts, so children were allowed to play in the streets and it was quite normal to see toddlers in the care of their older brothers and sisters all playing at marbles and suchlike. I was encouraged to play in our garden; a large piece of ground with a box tree summer-house, paths of low box hedging and lavender, an orchard at one corner, all offering plenty of places to play hide-and-seek. The laurel trees made splendid camps. This was to end, much to our disappointment, as father had been encouraged to use this land for building, as houses of the type suggested were needed for those retiring from business etc. So it was that the site was prepared for four nice houses and it was decided that we would move out of the shop into the first house once it was finished, and this eventually is what transpired. The large shop known as "The Cotswold Stores" was sold and the place which held so much mystery for me and all its pleasant memories of Christmas was to go. I never did walk the hidden stairway or secret tunnel which led from the basement of the shop to the parish church.

In due course the first house was finished and we were installed; a telephone exchange for this part of Gloucestershire, namely the Northleach area, was needed, so an extra room was allocated for this purpose in our house. It was a day and night service, managed by mother and father, and was a great source of interest for me. Lots of local news came through and also calls for the police, fire-engine and doctor.

One call for the fire-engine was from the village of Turkdean: a Dutch barn was on fire and the fire-engine at Andoversford was already out, so father, in his way, strapped a fire extinguisher to his motor bike and set off to assist. He was actually on the roof of the barn and using the extinguisher through the trapdoor on to the hay, when another fire appliance arrived. Father's extinguisher was empty, so they called him down to the ground to relieve him as there was little he could do. He then returned home and it was there that he realised the crêpe soles of his shoes had melted and separated from the uppers. So much for trying to help! *The Cheltenham and Gloucester Echo* referred to the unknown man who left the scene, smothered in black and rather scorched without giving his name. Just like my father!

Another call was from a large house out near the village of Sherborne. A prowler had been seen at the rear of the house and the housekeeper had phoned the Northleach police. The sergeant received the call and said that he had no one to send but would go himself. Father suggested he could accompany him, so in a few moments the sergeant turned up on his motor bike and sidecar. Off they went and after about half an hour they arrived a little way from the house. They left the motor bike combination off the road, and it was then suggested that the sergeant would approach the front door and father would circle the house to the back. Eventually, father found a poor old tramp asleep in one of the stables. He left him there and joined the sergeant over a cup of tea in the house. The old tramp was later woken up and taken into the workhouse at Northleach for the remainder of the night.

One evening I could not help hearing my mother and father discussing America and the money market, all above my head, but I was later to learn that a market had collapsed. They called it Wall Street.

Mother later explained that father had sold Cotswold Stores to help towards the cost of building the houses but it seemed there was little could be done to save the farm, the butcher's shop and the houses — father was bankrupt. It meant little to me at my age and it was years after I was made aware of what had really happened. But I was old enough to see the transformation in the home, the agonising look of painful despair on my mother's and father's faces. Only years after was I to realise the loss they had suffered.

The hard work of many years, not just a few hours each day, but often into the night preparing for the journeys next day — all gone in a matter of weeks. I still did not realise how serious our position was. Mother told us children that we would be moving home, that I should have to leave the grammar school and I would have to leave my gran and many pals. I presumed my sisters were in the same predicament and like me, knew not where we would go.

Everything seemed so mysterious. Then on the last Saturday evening in October, my sisters went to stay with granny. As the evening drew on, mother placed baby brother in his pram and moved out on to the path leading from the house to the pavement. I saw father come out of the house, turn and lock the door behind him. He placed the key in an envelope, straightened his shoulders, walked past mother and me, crossed the road and dropped the envelope through the letter-box of the bank.

I seemed to hear from father a sound as if he were about to cry. As he turned from the bank, his lips quivered but looking ahead he joined us and silently we moved through the market-place to the little square known as "The Green". I noticed that father and mother had donned their overcoats over their white shop coats. Father carried a solitary paper carrier bag containing the baby's clothes and feeding bottle. These were our only possessions except I had seen mother place the business ledger from the shop and some papers at the bottom of the pram. This ledger would provide mother with letter and notepaper in later days.

Conscious of prying eyes, of those who had seen the collapse of father's business, we moved on until we reached the cottage belonging to one of our old faithful customers, a kindly lady who had promised mother and baby a bed for the night. I, of course, returned to Granny Hyde's but unfortunately father was to spend a cold and miserable night on the back seat of a car that was parked at the rear of the local coal merchants.

Years after he had told us how through the long hours of the night, listening to the wind and rain, he had felt at breaking point, utterly lost and cursing himself for allowing himself to be drawn in to the business of building the four houses in order to satisfy his supposed council friends. He had also hoped that the sale of the houses would clear his mortgage and loan, and make life a little easier for mother. Unfortunately, the dreams had evaporated into thin air, leaving only recrimination and heart-break.

The next day being Sunday, we all met at Granny Hyde's and on her meagre ten shillings widow's pension she prepared a dinner for us, and in the afternoon father planned to scout around for accommodation for the family. Borrowing a bicycle, he managed to visit many of the outlying farms, and after two days of searching he eventually met a farmer who had been a very good customer of ours.

The farmer had one cottage vacant in a row of four and said we could have it as he did not intend to engage another worker. He said that the cottage had been empty for some time and would need some good fires to air the place. The cottage was some miles out from Northleach, but both mother and father seemed to be pleased. It appeared we were to look on this cottage as a haven away from gossip and false friends. It would be sad to leave dear Granny Hyde but we knew we could visit her when once we were settled in our new and exciting cottage in the country.

Much planning was done around granny's tea table. What to do about furniture and the little things that make up a home? We children wondered what we would play with. I had lost my pedal car; Peggy had lost her large doll's pram, doll's house, and dolls; everything down to my *Tiger Tim Christmas Annual* all went in the sale. Fortunately, I had left my comic papers with granny, there were my favourite *Comic Cuts*, *Chips*, *Rainbow*, and *Tiger Tim*. I was glad we could take these with us as both Peggy and Pat were able to read them to the younger ones.

When would we move? Who would help us?

This was decided when we had a visit from dear old Uncle Bob. "Be ready by ten o'clock on Saturday morning," he said, and went on to explain that he had also some furniture he had collected for us; and true to his word he had a full load, and we could sort it out when we reached the cottage. Granny had collected bedclothes and what food she could beg, borrow or steal for us.

Uncle Bob asked mother to climb onto the seat of the cart. Father went ahead on his bicycle while we children and the baby in the pram walked behind.

We left granny at the gate and made for the road off to the right that would take us out into the country lane and past the village of Eastington and on into the countryside that we were going to get to know so well over the years to follow.

I looked back at the town and in the road opposite the old workhouse I saw granny waving to us from her gate. I did not look back again until we had ascended the hill to the east of the town. From here I looked back over a town that had had its pleasant times but also a lot of heart-break. I then looked at my father who had stopped to look back and I can now understand why tears had flown. Then with head bowed he walked on almost in a daze. I had seen him as a stern man at times, a soldier indeed on Armistice Sunday, sometimes a quarrelsome man, yet loving and most kind to us, to the elderly and the unemployed. He was completely fearless but was for the moment a broken man and I am sure mother suffered in the same way, feeling the shame and bitterness. However, mother was a fighter and from the cart she called us to come on, one day we will come back, meanwhile, we were going to have some good times and she felt sure that we may even enjoy the country.

Father too, was leaving his few true friends and had little hope of playing billiards again with a professional named Davis who came to Northleach to do exhibition matches, or to share an evening drink with the Prince of Wales, who stopped in Northleach at the Union

Hotel on his way down to Wales where he was much loved by the Welsh. Father had met him in Flanders while serving with the Royal Army Medical Corps in 1916 on the Western Front, so there were many reminisences of those days in the mud and blood in France.

I had heard father say, "How in the world could this happen to me," but it was not his burden alone; mother too, had lost almost everything, and it would require much love, patience, determination, to overcome our predicament.

Meanwhile, we had been moving on the long winding dusty road, the horse and cart a little way ahead as we passed the high wall of a parkland known as Lodge Park, with tall beech trees in a continuous belt all around it, which seemed to stretch right over the horizon and everything seemed so large to us children.

Away over to the right, Uncle Bob pointed his whip to some small buildings standing in a corner of the fields away in the distance. One could just see the roofs of the farm and its cottages. Of course there were several fields and a copse between the buildings and us, which made them appear like toys.

We took the next fork road to the right and came across two cottages nestling in a little valley at the side of a copse. This was called Trowel Copse and a most delightful family lived there and they all became our friends in the years to come. Over the little valley we could see the cottage to which we were making. We turned into a lane on the right which would take us to our country cottage.

BROADFIELD FARM

NOT TO SCALE

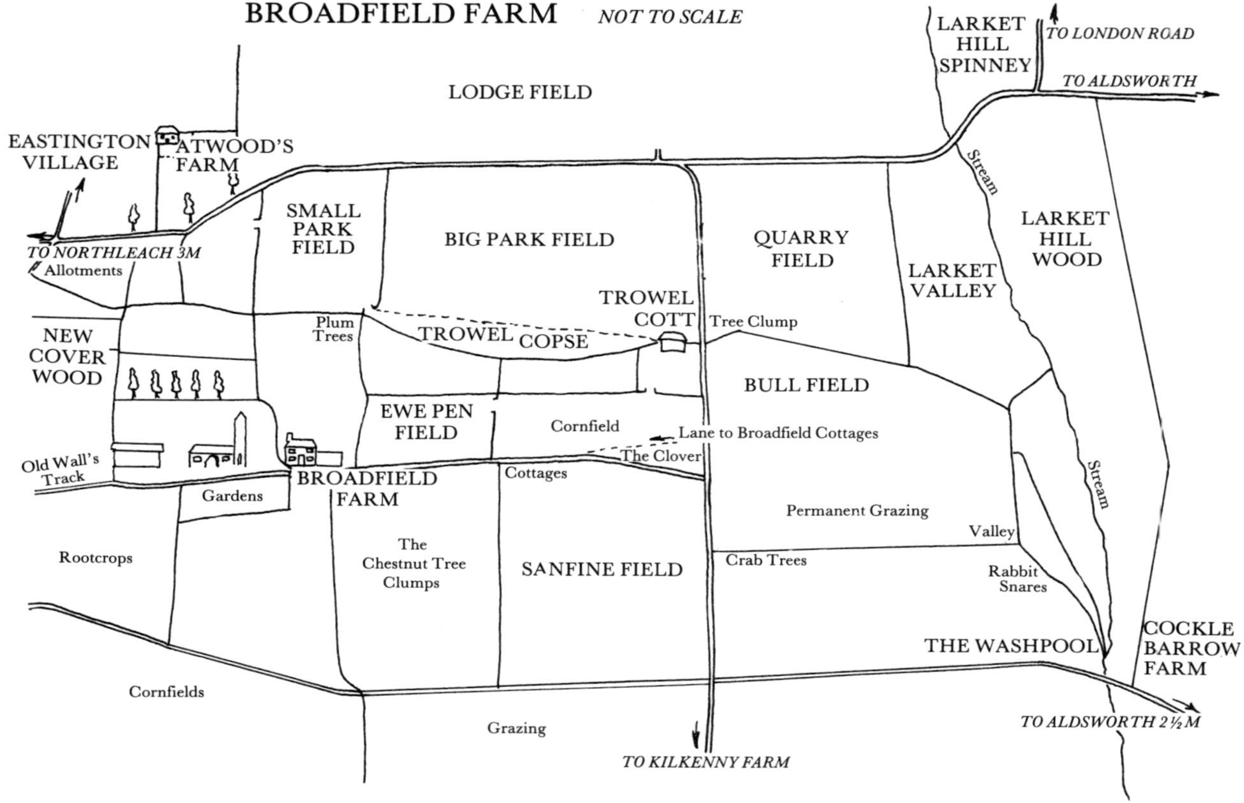

CHAPTER 5

A Place To Dream

This was Broadfield, a farm that was going to be our home for the next few years. We came to the four Cotswold stone built cottages first, all attached and all of identical size and appearance. Ours was the first in the row and we walked down the long garden path into a fairly large porch then into a large living-room having a large iron fireplace with a wide hearth and chimney-breast.

While uncle and father unloaded the cart, with a little assistance from me, the girls were exploring the house and from their excited chatter, it sounded as if they were going to like their new home. The cottage contained another room off the living-room which could have been a sitting-room if ever we found furniture for it. Off this room, there was a large scullery with a huge copper boiler in the corner, there was also a back-door which led to the outside toilet and a large shed in which we would store our wood etc.

We had three bedrooms and two attics which became our play rooms. All our windows faced across the fields, woods and valleys of this 2,000 acre farm. It was a sheep farm mainly and so it was mostly grassland.

The farmhouse stood within a large belt of beech and ash trees, with the farm buildings stretched out beyond the house and its large kitchen garden. There were all sorts of barns, sheds and horse stalls, so it looked as if there would be plenty to explore. The farm and its land belonged to what was known as the Sherborne Estate, a most beautiful estate with many villages, hamlets, and farms. To me at my age it was a world all of its own, thousands of miles as I saw it and too wide to walk across. How my mind worked trying to understand something that was going to be a new experience for all of us.

We were pleased that the weather was fine for our move and after the cart was unloaded uncle left us to settle in saying that he would return in a few days with what items he could collect on our behalf.

How fortunate for us that we had uncle to help us, inspite of the fact that he was a cripple, he worked so hard and mother's other brothers were not in evidence of course since they were most likely too far away or something. After uncle had departed we searched the shed for bits of wood so that we could have a fire to help warm the house. Mother boiled the water on a paraffin stove, so before long we were enjoying a cup of tea. It was while we were thus engaged that the farm manager came to the door to welcome us. The farm owner had told him of our plight and had decided to do all he could to help us. His name was Mr Wilson. We learned that his family consisted of his wife, a daughter Alice, and two boys, Willy and Duncan. What a great family they were too. Mr Wilson said that we were welcome to collect wood from the copse and the other woods on the farm and he laughingly said that if a rabbit should fall dead at our feet we should bring it home for the pot, since there were far too many eating the crops and killing all the small saplings that had been planted around the farm. Mrs Wilson came shortly after with some milk for which we were most grateful, she and mother were to become great friends in the days to follow.

After dad and I had helped mother sort out the bedroom things it was more like home, certainly not like the home we had left behind and more like camping out. There was a double bed in mother and father's room; a double bed for the three girls and myself who lay on the foot of the bed. My youngest sister and baby brother on an iron cot in mother's room. One day I was going to have my own room once we had more bedroom furniture.

We had a pleasant weekend, my sister Pat and I went to the wood to forage for dry trees that were laying all over the place. There were long larch trees that had been blown down and it did not take us long to collect two tall ones, and return home. We made several journeys for wood, marvelling at the amount that was there for us to collect. Fir cones were also in good supply and gave off a lovely smell of pine when burning.

Father said that he would walk back into Northleach to see Granny Hyde to let her know how we were fairing and to make enquiries with regard to applying for unemployment benefit. This, he was denied, due to the fact that he had been self-employed. It was rather ironical that the man that furnished him with this information, had a few years earlier suggested that father might stand for the mayorship of the town. He was still friendly and said that he was sorry, the best advice that he could give was to allow the parish to keep his wife and children; but to qualify for this, father would have to leave the family and seek work away. He was kindly told that if he valued this

The author standing with sister and nanny — June 1921

Thomas Arthur Tingley and Elsie Amelia Tingley — 1940

The author at 21 years, 1940.
In the Royal Army Medical Corps

President of Wantage Royal British Legion — 1986

magnanimus offer he must not return otherwise all relief would cease. With much saddness my father returned home with this awful news.

Mother did her best to explain to us children why father was going away. It was arranged that father would leave for London on the Wednesday morning, where he hoped one of his brothers would help him to find work.

In later years father was to tell us of this journey he had taken, not an easy time to say the least, as of course he had no money to pay for transport or food. He was grateful to a lorry driver in Oxford who gave him a sandwich, a drink of cold tea and a cigarette. Then by walking and hitch-hiking he reached London. The two days on the road left him tired and in need of a bath. He said that he was allowed to freshen up and stay the night with his elder brother.

Father eventually found an old friend in Southend-on-Sea who had served in the army with him. He was invited to stay and work for them. At first they were most kind, but soon it became quite evident that they were going to make the most of his experience as a grocer and he would be an asset to their business. A "God-given gift of a servant" a woman was heard to remark one day, but they were paying him well for his service, twelve shillings and sixpence a week. There was little left each week after paying five shillings towards his keep. Father wrote to us each week asking us to keep our peckers up, as this was his favourite expression.

I remember the excitement when mother read a letter from him saying that he had saved a few shillings and soon he would try to get home to see us. Some weeks later a letter came to tell us that father was coming home to see us, no one had to know about this of course, so the little ones were instructed not even to talk about it, since if our secret was told to the Council and Parish Council Officers, all help in the way of 'parish relief' would have been withheld. Father had planned to leave London on a charabanc which travelled down the Great West Road to Cheltenham. The charabanc left on time and father alighted at the crossroads between Northleach and the town of Burford. It was late evening and father walked the three miles home in the dark. Several times he was forced to leave the road and wait in the hedgerow until either a bicycle or the odd car had passed by. Walking over the fields as a short cut father was able to creep up to the side of the house and then when all was clear he crept round and into the porch — three knocks and he was inside. After embracing each of us in turn, he turned to mother and I felt there were tears of relief as at last father was at home. In the glimmer of candle-light father enjoyed a cup of tea and bread and dripping, his favourite.

Then the stories of his adventure were told; it was all awe-inspiring to us children. We were still in the vacuum of this new world into which we had been brought, thrilling in some ways to us, but little realising how terribly painful and serious it was for mother and father. We were far too young to appreciate the enormity of what had really transpired in such a short period. Whispers at first of a 'general strike'; gossip of the collapse of the money-market, business men like father losing everything; people in desperation taking their own lives; it was no wonder that mother said we children should say our prayers and thank God that both she and father had a spiritual strength which would help them through the crisis.

The weekend flew past and in the dusk of Sunday evening father said his farewells and crept off across the fields. I went with him until we reached the road. We had been able to talk together in muffled tones because voices carry at night. Father turned to me before climbing over the wall to reach the road, he embraced me, then with a pat on my head he said, "Do your best my boy, look after your mother, see you again soon."

Then in silence he disappeared up Larket Hill from where he would have to walk about two miles to catch his charabanc. With tears in my eyes I turned for home. By now it was dark, but on nimble feet I trotted over the fields dodging sheep that were either laying or grazing and they would move to one side when they heard the padding of my plimsoles as I passed them in the night. Eventually the light of the cottage came in to view.

Monday morning came and it was all get up and go — carry sufficient wood in for mother then a quick wash and then we three older ones started out for the school in the village of Aldsworth some two or three miles away. This was our first day and we walked along with the Wilson children who introduced us to the teachers and other children. We were to remember those days, it was hardly light when we would start out in the mornings and we often arrived wet and dishevelled at school. The teacher would give us sheets of brown paper to stuff down our trousers. My sisters would hang their dresses over the fire-guards to dry out and we lads would stand around the stove to get warm. Summer days it was often quite pleasant but the winters were absolutely terrible. Of course if the snow was too deep as often it was, we would remain at home, this was better than having to strip off in front of the class, which often caused tittering. Most children went home for dinner, a number brought sandwiches but we Tingleys were given four Osborne biscuits each for lunch; but often these were eaten on the way to school, in case they became sodden with the damp clothes. We were sometimes priviledged to purchase a mug of Horlicks or Ovaltine for a halfpenny when mother had been able to save a few coppers from the five shillings father had saved for her.

We soon accepted the schoolmaster and teacher who also seemed to have accepted us children. We enjoyed the lessons and often asked for homework for the weekends when the days were longer. There was little point in having homework in the winter months as it was almost dark when we arrived home in the afternoon and my time seemed to be spent collecting wood and the remainder of the evening was spent in candle-light.

Of course there were times when our lives were not so happy at school and that was when one family of rather large lads of the village took a dislike to me and for some unknown reason they became quite spiteful. They would waylay us on the way home and the result was a bloody nose and bruises. We would stop at a little brook before we reached home and wash my face or else mother would ask questions. She was utterly against us children fighting, but we could not hide anything from her and she said that father would give me boxing lessons when he returned home so that I could make a better effort of defending not only myself but my sisters also, since they were just as vulnerable as I, especially where larger teenagers were concerned. So until father was able to come home again we would keep an eye out for our antagonisers and often return home by a different route. It was farther to go but it was more peaceful and on the way we passed a shepherd's hut on wheels in a field where the sheep were confined ready for lambing. While a friend kept watch I guiltily entered the hut and found sacks of maize and locust beans for the sheep. So it was that the locust beans were enjoyed on the remainder of our journey home. It was almost dark when we clambered over the stone wall into the wood of Larket Hill, landing in a deep bed of beech leaves. As we jumped down, we set to flight lots of pheasants. A slight scare for the moment but realising we had arrived on our own land we felt more secure.

Away to our right near the road, was a small hollow at the side of the stream. Many times we espied the flickering flames of a fire. A lonely tramp would often spend the night there, so it was wise for us to make our way quietly down through the wood trying not to break dead branches, which would echo through the trees. The wood was quite dense in one place and the pheasants did not take kindly to being disturbed having just gone to roost. The noise they made when taking to the wing must have scared every creature and the tramp also, although I dare say the sights and the sounds of the countryside did not worry him.

With father away, we gradually got into a routine at the cottage. Mother, not enjoying very good health, was very often forced to remain in bed. We older ones took it in turn to remain at home and care for mother making the fire and keeping the place fairly warm for when mother came down to advise us in the preparation of food for the girls on their return from school.

I was allowed to have Friday off school since it was my job to walk to Northleach to collect the 'parish relief'. I would leave home around eight o'clock in the morning although we did not really know the correct time for our alarm clock was very old. It had a bell on top and had a friendly rhythm to its gentle ticking as it stood on the mantelshelf. Although I hurried across the fields to the road at Lodge Park I arrived at Granny Hydes with just enough time to have a drink of tea and a slice of toast before presenting myself outside the relieving office for nine o'clock. So there I was, a lad of twelve, school cap tied on with a scarf often against the winter's blast, still in short trousers, fairly lanky for my age, waiting to face the awesome spectre that would take my name then disappear inside. I had joined the queue at a few minutes to nine. I was the only child present and felt out of place amongst the elderly men and women waiting for the hand-out. I saw one after another receive their little chit of paper for food or fuel and I was actually at the door when I heard the man inside go for coffee. On his return, he stepped outside and beckoned to an elderly woman behind me saying, "I am sure this young man won't mind me doing the older ones first."

I received a nice pat on the head and I stood to one side and of course one after another, old folk shuffled past to receive their alms. I was surprised at how quickly the morning had flown and at one o'clock I heard the door close. This was the chance I needed and I would hasten to granny's for a cup of soup and crusty bread, something I had looked forward to while standing out in the street. I expect old gran worried when I once again returned to wait for my turn to receive the little piece of paper that meant so much to my family. If my benefactor was in a good mood I would eventually be called inside. The office was warm and I could understand why the door opened and closed so swiftly.

Grasping my slip of paper I would hurry to the little shop down the street where I would collect the usual essentials. Two pounds of margarine, two pounds of sugar, two pounds of dried peas, three pounds of flour, two packets of tea, one pound of lard, cocoa, six candles, and last but not least a box of matches, and if the lady had any cheap bacon pieces, mother would be pleased.

I would then return to granny's where she had a large hessian shopping bag packed with cottage loaves and a large basin of beef dripping, which was kindly sent to us once a fortnight by the headmaster's wife at the college. After a warm cup of tea and a nice slice of buttered toast I would load up the bags I had on to a stick over my shoulder. Granny bade me take care and I would start on my way home. I had been delayed so long at the P.R. Office that the day had passed and the evening dusk had begun to close in as I moved out of Northleach along the country lanes. It would be dark for most of the journey and I would meet cyclists with their little carbide lamps flickering as they passed by. Sometimes there would be a brief 'goodnight' to which I would reply. Often there was little or no exchange. The local policeman always called, 'goodnight son', to my boyish goodnight.

I was so pleased to get home to remove my outer clothes which were usually wet, it being November. I would bring more wood in for the fire so that my damp clothes could be draped around it through the night. To save the little paraffin we had for the small oil lamp, we would all go to bed and lay and tell stories until eventually the voices would gradually cease. I remember feeling pleased that I had been able to help mother by going to Northleach and to save her the embarrassment of almost begging for assistance.

CHAPTER 6

The Visitation

Winter came early, and long before Christmas, the countryside was covered with snow which grew deeper as the days passed. We were pleased and encouraged when mother said we should begin to make our plans for Christmas. The plans consisted of making lists of presents which we would like Father Christmas to bring us.

We older children had the job of keeping the wood supply going. Pat and I would saw logs out in the shed and then Peggy and Betty would carry the logs in and make a good pile in the scullery, and at the side of the fireplace in the living-room. Potatoes, swedes and turnips which we had scrounged from the fields were brought in away from the frosts. Mother kept her eye on our provisions and said that before the snow got too deep we should visit the field where the sheep were feeding on swedes. So with a sack we sallied forth to replenish our stocks. We made a good meal from boiled swede with bread and margarine.

Mother remarked that it was a pity we had no Christmas tree but Pat and I did something to remedy that, and in the dusk of the evening we entered Trowel Copse where we broke a large branch off a yew tree which covered us in snow. Nevertheless, we pulled the branch home and after shaking the snow off, we took it in to the living-room and stood it against the wall.

The younger girls had finished their lists and they attempted to dress the tree with different items, such as ladies in different forms of dress from a woman's catalogue. It was so exciting to see the tree with streamers of newspaper advertising toys, household goods and clothes, and providing no one pulled too much, the branch would remain upright.

Our last meal before bed was dripping toast, if the fire allowed it, even the baby could suck on a piece of dripping crust. As stated before, the dripping came from the headmaster's wife at the college.

She was most kind to mother and us children since she remembered us from better times and felt for us in our need.

As usual, we spent the early part of the evening sitting around the flickering fire, with mother in the armchair telling us of her Christmases at home as a girl. We were always enthralled by her stories she told which added to the atmosphere of Christmas and found that the evening had passed away quite quickly. The baby was asleep on mother's knee, my sister Rose was leaning against Pat and there was every sign that the candle should be lit and we should go to bed. These were indeed exceptional times so there was no hurry. This was Christmas Eve and we still believed that tomorrow all would be well. Mother had said that God in his love would be with us and grant all we prayed for.

Mother said we could manage for a day or two as we still had a cottage loaf, margarine and potatoes and swedes. Yes, we would be all right, in any case the snow might have gone in the morning allowing Pat and I to walk to Granny Hyde's for some food. Not only that, but Father Christmas would be able to get through with the presents we had asked for. The lists incidentally had been thrown up the chimney so that they would float up to where Father Christmas lived. In the flickering flames from the fire we gazed at our poor but wonderful Christmas tree with its coloured paper leaning sadly to one side against the living-room wall. Yet, in its simplicity it was a part of the mystery and wonder of Christmas.

Christmas morning came with a dark and dismal sky. All the windows were covered with frost, it had been a terribly cold night. The snow had not gone, large flakes were still falling. I became conscious of movement from mother's room and after a short while I heard her rise. She moved across the room in the gloom and as she descended the stairs I heard her crying quietly. I could not understand why anyone should cry on Christmas morning. Then I heard mother in her desperation say, "Oh God help us!" It was a cry for help from a mother with the responsibility of six children with little or no food to feed us after today, and if there had been any money the weather would prevent us getting out to the road, let alone the three and a half miles to Northleach. It was in later years that I began to understand in some small way the feeling of desolation and helplessness that had wrung from mother that cry of, "Oh God help us!"

I was about to get dressed and go down stairs to help mother when I heard her ascending the stairs. She had by now composed herself for the sake of the children and I expect she had decided to put on a brave face as she had said her faith in her Heavenly Father had renewed her strength. She knew He never forsook those who loved and trusted

Him. On numerous occasions her words of comfort and encouragement would be remembered by us children.

Having washed and done her hair, she put on her little apron of Paisley design with its patch pocket holding her handkerchief which had certainly had more than its fair use, since tears had been many but usually hidden from us children. I dread to think of what mother's thoughts and feelings must have been with no husband to share those lonely nights, although I fully expect that father was suffering also, realising our situation and mother's sorrow.

Mother had lit the fire in the living-room so that it would be a little warmer when we children came down. How cold it must have been for her dear hands endeavouring to get the wood to burn after fumbling around in the scullery for the few sticks for kindling, although we youngsters spent time twisting paper into spills for the fire. Of course, very often if I had left a good fire at night it was sometimes still red in the morning.

Now mother appeared at the door into our bedroom singing in her soft voice the first bars of *Away in a manger, no crib for a bed.* Then she said, "Come on you lazy children, Father Christmas has been with the first presents and he is coming back later with more." With these words she gave each of us a small newspaper packet in which we found the last of mother's dried fruit, with which she had meant to make a cake. We were asked not to eat them too quickly and make them last until Father Christmas came back.

So we all helped each other dress and went down to the living-room. We only had one cold tap in the scullery, so washes were not too frequent. After a short while, I set about getting in more wood. My sister Pat, was doing jobs for mother whilst my eldest sister Peggy, was given the job to spy out the land as mother said. Peggy knelt on the high window seat to watch for anyone coming up the road, especially Father Christmas. We did not usually have visitors, except of course the school attendance officer from time to time, and that was in fine weather not in weather such as we had now; it was awful and we had little hope of Father Christmas returning.

It was about midday when Peggy gave a cry and said, "I've seen a large black cat on the wall near the gate."

Mother said, "Good, that means good luck, go on Bern you have a look."

This I did and as I peered through the icy window I saw not a black cat, but a black bowler hat, held on to a person's head, with a scarf. The person was endeavouring to open the gate but this was impossible, due to the height of the snow. In desperation, the person who appeared to be of small build, threw a large sack over the gate then squeezed through to stumble down the path. All this information

I passed back to mother, who had begun to pat her hair down and straighten her pinafore. After a few moments, the apparition succeeded in forcing his way through the snow, which was up to his waist, into our porch. We heard him stamping his feet, then there came a muffled knock at the door. Mother signalled me to draw the bolt and open the door. Then from the depth of the clothing covering the person's face, came the greeting, "Morning Mrs Tingley. A happy Christmas to you and the children."

The voice came from a gentleman of smallish build, a voice that held warmth and sincerity, a voice we came to recognise and respect in the following years.

"Oh do come in Mr Green," said mother who immediately recognised the gentleman from Northleach; he was well known as the local sanitary inspector and had known mother and father for a number of years.

Our guest asked how we were faring, and how father was, and did we have enough food. All these questions were soon answered by mother who explained our situation. Of course, while this conversation was taking place we children, not daring to move in case we broke the spell, kept our eyes on the large sack on the floor and on the gentleman who had left his warm home on Christmas day to bring us the sack of mysteries which lay at his feet. There was the odd sniff as six children with runny noses listened to his story.

He and his family had gone to morning mass and the priest had said, "If any of you good people out of the goodness of your hearts should think of anyone who may be in need at this Christmas time, please give, if only a little to lighten and brighten someone's Christmas." Apparently these good folk had shared similar thoughts and decided that they had enough to spare and more, so it was agreed that Mr Green would do his best to reach us. How he did that journey I shall never know, especially with a sack of its size on his shoulders in such weather. He too must have had a deep sense of love for his fellow man. A Christian without a doubt. We were never to have a Christmas without thinking of Mr Green and his family, who showed such a wealth of compassion to us. Thanks be to God.

Then our visitor said that he ought to make a start back for Northleach as the skies were so grey and darkness would come early. He declined a cup of tea from mother; he must have thought that it would have taken too long to boil a kettle on the fire which had been forgotten in the excitement and had reduced to embers. Adjusting his clothes, putting on his wellingtons and tying on his bowler hat, he made his way to the door. Wishing mother and us a very happy Christmas again, he promised to see us in the new year and with a wave of his hand, and saying "God bless you," he disappeared up the garden path, just as silently and mysteriously as he had arrived. No one spoke as I climbed on to the window seat to see if I could see anything of Mr Green, but he had gone, we hoped, to enjoy Christmas with his loved ones.

It was mother's voice which brought me back to the floor and I heard her saying, "Well of all things! Fancy Mr Green of all people thinking of us. His Christian act was certainly an answer to my prayers, I asked God for help and he did. Come on Bern, help me to lift this sack on to the table please."

So with six enquiring faces watching every move I made, I undid the string at the neck of the sack. Mother opened the sack and drew out a large piece of fruit cake, a piece of boiled bacon, half a pound of butter, there were also oranges, nuts, a large bag of fruit drops, some children's books and a bundle of comic papers. Wonders of wonders this was indeed Christmas. Mother was most careful with each item, we each had a boiled sweet, the first for months. The fire was made up and the flames began to flicker around the room. The atmosphere had changed from gloom, to one of the joy of anticipation as we thought of the wonderful food which lay on the pantry shelves. What luxuries we would now be able to enjoy. The late afternoon was spent helping mother arrange tea. I built up the fire as was my job. Peggy looked after the two younger children and Pat helped mother who said that we could spare two candles for the mantelshelf, as it was Christmas, and one in the neck of a sauce bottle in the middle of the kitchen table. All was set for the meal, which we had longed for, hoped for and prayed for. We each had a slice of toast spread with beef dripping followed by a nice slice of fruit cake and a mug of milky tea, what a feast.

Later, having cleaned the table and blown two candles out, we all drew around mother near the fire, giving thanks to Granny Hyde who had spent long winter evenings making us a large cloth mat which lay in front of the fireplace. She had also begged a piece of coconut matting which covered half the living-room. I remember carrying home a thin carpet which mother kept for special occasions, such as when our neighbour from across the fields came. Mother had this nice carpet in her bedroom for when our guest was invited to see the bedrooms. While our guest inspected the attic we promptly removed the imitation Persian carpet, took it downstairs and spread it over the old table in the living-room. It looked fine, just like a real table cover. I often wondered if our guest rumbled us because our little escapade was not without a certain amount of whispering. However, our plan seemed to work thanks to mother's effort to impress one who seemed to have everything inspite of the shortages. Her husband was a farm labourer who collected fifteen shillings a week. Our guest from across the fields was a good manager and mother too, having four children. The eldest boy was a great pal of mine, we called him snowball.

Our guests' children were well-behaved and helped look after the fire out under the plum tree where all the cooking was done during the spring and summer months. This certainly reduced house cleaning and there was plenty of fuel for the fire because their house rested in the lee of the copse. Unfortunately, we had to carry or drag the wood for our fire over two fields and through several gates to reach home.

So it was on Christmas night we sat and listened to mother telling us stories of long ago. Wonderful fairy stories, biblical stories and the story of her life in business. Mother would sometimes refer to her family and the history behind her father's name. He was Robert Hyde who was descended from the Hydes of the time of James I. Mother was the youngest daughter, and thinking back over the years, I have to admit there were times when she seemed to have had certain regret when she gave up her family name of Hyde from possibly Lady Amelia to a plain Mrs. Not that she regretted marrying dad, but this was at the cost of losing her family's affection, as her marriage caused much displeasure. There was so much dissension in her family. Father was looked on with jealousy and suspicion despite his generosity to my grandparents and relations with food parcels when they were a bit short as they claimed. We older children were able to remember mother's stories in years to come.

So Christmas passed and a new year was born. The snow had slowly disappeared to be followed by rain. We older children went to school as often as possible and received a fair and comprehensive education considering the times and size of the school. It was wonderful and well managed by the headmaster and teachers.

The weather had prevented me from lifting swedes from under the huge bury, which contained not only swedes, but mangels and potatoes. Well covered with straw and earth it lay underneath a hedge in one of the fields near the farm. It would have been unwise of me to dig into the pit in case the frost penetrated and that would have ruined the whole winter store of animal fodder.

On the Sunday morning, mother had said that the few potatoes we had, had been used up and would I go to the farm to see if there were any left in the grain shed, but unfortunately my visit drew a blank, so I had to return to tell mother that our only hope was if Mrs Wilson had a few potatoes to spare. Mother and I noticed that it had begun to snow again so I said I would go out and try to catch a rabbit, something I was getting fairly good at; well I thought so, but I had only caught one before. The poor creature had taken refuge in a wall and I had learned from the manager's son how to listen for movement, then having located the rabbit pull a stone out of the wall as near as possible to the rabbit. Then thrusting one hand in, grab hold and draw it out squealing which rather upset me, nevertheless, the family needed food and I intended to supply some.

Before I left for my walk, mother said she would visit Mrs Wilson while I kept an eye on the children and cut a few more logs. We would need a good fire as the snow was still falling heavily and we were heading for a cold night. At mother's knock, I unbolted the back-door to hear that Mrs Wilson had only enough potatoes for her own needs but would ask her husband to collect some from the pit as soon as the weather permitted.

Mother and I returned to the living-room to join the children and to discuss what we should do. Mother suggested that we had a cup of tea as it would help us to think better. Saying this over her shoulder, she made for the scullery to get the kettle. Then I heard an exclamation from her and she returned to the door and said, "Who came while I was at the Wilsons?"

I said, "No one had, why?"

"Come and look, there's a sack on the copper, so someone has been," replied my mother.

Hurrying to her side, I saw the sack for myself and I could actually feel that it contained potatoes. But no one had entered the scullery this I proved to mother by going to the back-door and pointing to one set of footprints in the snow being mother's when she had gone to the Wilsons.

Once again, we had proof of answered prayers, and we were beginning to believe more than ever in God's goodness.

CHAPTER 7

With Care and with Stealth

Once the weather had improved, and mother was feeling stronger after the strain of winter, she said that she felt much better and she would walk into Northleach to see her mother. It would be the following Friday and mother said she would collect the 'parish relief', which meant that it would entail not only the long walk there, but also the long wait outside the relief office, and the heavy shopping bags to carry home. Mother said that I had spent too much time away from school, but if I hurried home after school I could go and meet her to help carry the bags.

This I agreed to do, because I realized I ought to try and learn as much as possible before leaving school in two years' time. Of course I always had a great desire to be at home to do my chores as I was most conscious of how much mother depended on me, especially the times when she had to spend time in bed when suffering with haemorrhage.

Unless one of us children stayed at home there was no one to make mother a drink, or to break the monotony of the long hours alone. There was little to see or hear except an occasional sound of horses' hooves on the road as a cart of fodder went into the fields for the sheep. Many times mother remarked how peaceful everything was, compared to the busy life she left behind at the shop.

I had to admit I had a great desire to remain at home to do a more practical job, rather than sit in a classroom all day. Yet I had to agree it was most important to get a good education, if we were going to return to Northleach and start a business once again. So I had every intention of learning the three Rs as mother put it. I might even do so well, that one day I would ascend to the dizzy heights of being a relieving officer, and replace the oversized gent in pin-stripes, who had so grudgingly handed out our weekly meal ticket. But I felt sure that with my birth, and experience, I would have had the good grace, not to inflict hardship, but to ease the already over-burdened mortals who came in all weather to collect their pittance.

Friday morning came and mother set off for Northleach as soon as us children had left for school, leaving sister Pat to care for the two younger ones. The visit to town was a nice change for mother, especially being able to spend a little time with her mother, Granny Hyde, and catch up with local gossip.

To mother's surprise it was not too embarrassing at the relief office; the man was quite polite with a little broader smile; but no increase in relief. I understand there was a certain amount of shame on mother's part, almost as if she had committed a terrible crime when holding out her hand, for a slip of paper which was held by a well-manicured hand; but it was always hard to interpret the grimace, or smile, which did nothing to improve her feelings.

It was dark before she concluded her business of collecting the food, etc. to bring home; so after a cup of tea with Granny Hyde, she donned her old mackintosh and headscarf and with a hurried goodbye to granny, mother stepped out into the evening dusk. The difficult start to the journey home, was to negotiate Mace Hill, fully loaded with shopping bags. It's quite a long haul to the summit where one could look back over the town, with its street lamps and windows beginning to shine through the mist that was rising in the valley. Mother was a woman of faith and had enormous courage and faced up to each day's problems usually with the words "All will be well, God is with us". I feel it was with this confidence that she stepped out bravely with the essential goods that would have to last until the following Friday, when it would be my turn to make the journey.

Mother had so many thoughts to occupy her mind as she continued her way, the first and foremost must have been the welfare of her children. It is quite possible that her mind may have been a little apprehensive for her own welfare considering the length of journey, and the lonely places she would have to pass; then there was the disquieting news of the poor woman who had been murdered recently on her way home from shopping in Northleach. Not on this actual road but one that ran parallel towards Burford.

Not the pleasantest of thoughts to carry with one, on such a night as this. I'm sure the road must have seemed endless, but apparently mother's walk had been quite pleasant, especially as one could see the little lights shining from the various windows of the cottages across the fields in the village of Eastington. Sometimes a feeling of the unknown would push itself to the fore, and as mother later said, "It made me quicken my steps towards home". The road eventually ran alongside the high wall of Lodge Park, with its high overhang of huge beech trees. It was terribly dark, and awfully lonely; sometimes an odd cyclist would pass, offering a cheery goodnight, others would pass in silence. But this was to be mother's last journey to Northleach on her own, firstly for her own safety, and secondly we did not realize it then, but our circumstances were going to change before very long, for the better.

So, having arranged to go and meet mother, I hurried home from school. I had to make sure that the fire was made up, and wood brought in for the night. The young ones were in the care of my sisters Peg and Pat and I waited long enough to hear the bolts on the front door pushed home.

The girls and I had grown up quite a bit in the last few months and had become used to being responsible for the younger ones. We also had begun to feel a part of this farm, and had got to know the few people who lived in the area. The woods, roads and fields, even in the dark, held little fear for my sister Pat and I; we had become quite familiar with the sights and sounds around our farm, and could identify such sounds. But if we had any doubts at all, then we would remain close to the ground, or behind a convenient bush until we were satisfied there was no one near us.

So it was that I set off across the farmland to meet mother. I made good time as I quickly trotted over the fields in my plimsoles, making little noise, except the swish of the long grass catching my legs as I hastened on. I skirted Trowel Copse in the valley, and crossed another field and found that I had judged my path very well, despite the fact that except for the stars it would have been totally dark. The moon had risen but was low on the horizon. I arrived beside the wall overlooking the road opposite the park, this was the road which mother would come along, I had no idea of the time, but settled down to wait close to the wall near a hawthorn tree. The wall was fairly low at this point and only a few feet from the edge of the road, and beyond the road was a wide grass verge and the ten-foot stone wall of Lodge Park, with the beech trees that seemed to ascend right up into the starry sky. So I waited in the shadows, listening for the prearranged signal from my mother, who in her soft contralto voice would sing the first few bars of the hymn *O God our help in ages past, our hope for years to come*. I was to whistle the remainder of the verse in answer.

I leaned closer to the wall as the odd cyclist passed by with their little flickering paraffin lamps on their cycle. As they disappeared, I wondered what they would have thought if they had known that a boy of my age had been watching them from the shadows.

I breathed freely once again, but still clutched my stick and was quite prepared to stand and wait, or if the need arose, I could run like the wind across the fields, away from any threat; but little would stop me from meeting mother.

I had been watching bats flying under the trees above my head and listening to the owls hoot in the park. I heard a vixen calling from across the fields and I thought that it was a dog fox that answered her from the larches in Trowel Copse. It was then that I thought I heard the sound of steps on the gravel of the road in the distance. Straining my ears I waited with bated breath, then at last I heard the faint sound of the familiar tune, and it was getting stronger as the singer came closer. I rose up and jumped over the wall and gaining the road I walked quickly towards mother whistling the remainder of the hymn; and from up the road, which was now bathed in moonlight, I heard mother call, "Is that you Bern?"

Answering in the affirmative, I went forward and relieved mother of one of the large shopping bags; then as usual we carried on walking and singing in quiet tones, to save our breath. We had perhaps gone a hundred yards or so, when to my horror the crouching form of a man rose up from beside the wall, where a few minutes earlier I had waited for mother. The figure slid over the wall, and bending double, hurried across the road less than a hundred yards in front of us. He then climbed the opposite wall and disappeared from view.

Mother and I did not falter in our singing, and continued walking. Mother gave no indication that she had seen anything, and without intending to alarm her I changed the shopping bag over to my left hand and clutched my stick firmly in my right hand. Then I turned about without faltering, and managed to walk backwards keeping pace with mother, who like myself continued singing showing no sign that she had seen anything unusual. I was able to keep an eye on the spot where the man had disappeared so was not surprised when I saw him rise up on the other side of a large ash tree which grew near to where he had jumped over the wall. I could see him quite plainly with the moonlight shining behind him, as he stood looking at us. I had no idea what he had in mind, but we were gradually putting distance between us, and I hoped that mother was still unaware of what had taken place. She had said nothing, and was still quietly singing hymns we both knew. I was in the process of turning around to walk normally, when we heard the voices of people coming along behind us from Northleach. It was two men on their bicycles; they were laughing and chatting together, and were about to pass us, when I called out "Hello, could you tell us the time please."

Both men stopped and dismounted from their cycles, and one opened his coat and pulled out his timepiece, looking at it in the light of his little paraffin headlamp. He said, "Well now, I guess it be nigh on Ah, pass six as near as damn it. Oh, sorry missus, I seed whom you be now," in typical Gloustershire brogue.

We walked on with them for some distance, glad of their company and for the protection it had given us. I said nothing of what I had seen, for mother's sake, so they knew nothing of the gratitude I really felt towards them. We came to the gate where we would cut across the fields for home, so with cheery goodnights they mounted their cycles and pedalled off into the evening moonlight. We always felt a certain amount of relief once we had got on to our own land, as we always called it.

Broadfield, was indeed our home in every sense. We loved and knew every inch of its thousands of acres. Mother was not quite as familiar with the woods as I was, so it was necessary for me to guide her with my hand past rabbit holes, dodging tree stumps, under low branches, as we proceeded over the field, through Trowel Copse, until we were out in the moonlight in the field beyond. Another fifteen minutes and we were at our backyard, and going round the side of the house we knocked on the front door with our signal. It was promptly opened by my sister Pat, who had watched for our return from an upstairs window.

Once again the door was closed and bolted. Only then did I breathe a sigh of relief, and said "Thank God," for the safety He had given us, and the security of our home.

I remember turning to look at mother who was in the process of removing her coat and headscarf. She sent an inquiring glance towards me, and I said, "It's all right now, Mum."

She said, "Are you all right, Bern?"

I said I was, but I could see a further questioning look, so I said, "Yes, Mum, I'm quite all right, we are safe home, and ready for a nice cup of tea. I expect you feel ready for one also."

Mother said, "Indeed I do. But tell me Bern, did you see anything strange along Park Road tonight?"

I said, "So you did see that man also. I wondered if you had, you did not say anything, but I kept an eye on him."

Mother said, "I thought you were very brave, and also jolly good at walking backwards; and the way you made your voice deeper to sound as if you were a man, that was good thinking. Nonetheless Bern, I was so pleased when those men caught us up, it was good to have them to talk to, until we were able to cross our land."

I thought perhaps mother had been amused by my actions, but I realised she really was pleased with me, and we were very pleased with each other's company that night to say the least. The situation could have been worse, and the outcome more serious, but thank God we were all safe at home.

Our conversation had reached the ears of the girls who naturally wanted to know what happened, so mother explained the evening's scary event, and proceeded to warn them not to delay on the road at night, when returning from school.

Peggy said "Why isn't father here to take care of us? Why doesn't he come home? Let's all write him a letter and tell him of that horrible man. It may have been the same man who killed poor Mrs Matthews of Sherborne?"

But mother said, "No, that man has been sent to prison. He won't do any more harm now. I think the man tonight was only a poor man trying to catch a few rabbits for his family."

This explanation seemed to satisfy Peggy, but no doubt the imagination would continue to work for some time to come. I am sure it proved to be a lesson to us all, to keep our eyes open, and to hurry home from school or if we were ever sent on an errand. The episode had certainly conjured up pictures of outlaws, brigands, and awful men who stole our rabbits.

My sister Pat, was not easily scared, and said, "We must make plans, in case any prowlers come round the farm."

We had two old carving knives in the kitchen; these were sharpened on the doorstep, and would be kept within easy reach; and the doors would be always bolted, while father was away.

Our escapade was the topic of conversation on many occasions, and certainly gave us serious thoughts in regard to the children's safety on their way to and from school; and they promised to always hurry home, especially on dark evenings. We were glad, that we had decided that mother would never go to Northleach on her own again. I would go myself, school or no school, until father returned home again to stay. Meanwhile we hoped and prayed it would be soon. In the following days I carried a nut stick and one of the old kitchen knives in my jacket.

By the age of thirteen I had become adept at throwing a flint stone, or my stick, and could hit a running rabbit at twenty paces. I did my share of running too, and beat most of the older lads at school sports. I was learning fast about the ways of the countryside, and with our recent experiences, once again I found my thoughts turning to father, wondering if he would be home for our next Christmas at Broadfield.

With the evenings still fairly dark, I had to saw wood by the light of a candle — our stocks had to be kept up. Mother was unable to cut wood, I was also the one to provide meat for the pantry. The farm foreman's son Willy, had shown me how to track rabbits and to set snares. I became quite proficient. I was very proud to be the man of the family, and killing for food became a duty, to fulfil the need of the family.

At different points on the farm, could be found my store of weapons, a roll of bag tie string, half a dozen flint stones, a couple of good nut sticks, all these were deposited under the rafters in a farm building, under a hayrick, or behind a blackberry bramble bush. I had a razor blade, some string and a book of matches in an OXO tin. These were in a rabbit hole, in the bank, just inside Larket Hill Wood, to the north of the farm. I would go out in the evening, and by creeping along the side of the walls of the fields adjacent to the wood, I could peep over the wall and watch the rabbits feeding, someway out in the field. I would interrupt their evening meal by jumping over the wall and in their haste to get away from my swinging stick they would scramble into the nearest hole in the wall. I would take note of the hole they used, and it became normal for them to use the same holes as a means of refuge, time after time. So I hastily thrust my arm into each hole, fumbling with my fingers until I felt the soft fur of the hiding rabbit. I would locate its back legs, and gradually pull the writhing body out; sometimes the poor furry creature would squeal. I did not achieve the knack of wringing necks until I was older, but I hastily dispatched the rabbit with a sharp blow of my stick behind its ears. I would often go home with two or three rabbits, but not without a sense of guilt, killing these lovely things of God's creation, and stealing from the land, despite having permission to catch rabbits from the farm foreman. Of course he said nothing about catching pheasants and partridges. But mother had need of meat. I did not miss the chance of anything, so when I took mother into the large pantry to see what was hanging there, she would say "Good Boy Bern, may God forgive us."

Then there was the time when Pat and I planned to get mother a change from rabbit and pheasants. Our walks to the wood for firing took us through a field where the pens were at lambing time; the field was called the Ewe Pens; it was here that the free-range chickens were kept. It was a great temptation to know that there were a large number of Rhode Island Red fowl roosting on their perches. Our visit to those feathered diners, had to be after the snow had gone. Otherwise we would leave tracks, so our visit would be delayed until spring. I had often followed the tracks of rabbits, and grew to know the different bird signs. I also knew when a fox had made a recent kill. Spots of moist blood and a few feathers told of a swift killing, and a hurried return to its cubs in the wood known as New Cover. This was a large wood of larch trees and hazel-nut, surrounded with its dense undergrowth. The keeper's ride, was a few yards inside the wood, and circled the whole area. The keeper was able to walk round the wood, without being seen from the outside and his presence was only realized when various birds sounded the alarm.

One evening mother went with us to collect blackberries from the hedge adjacent to New Cover, when I noticed a rabbit in one of my snares, it was struggling to rid itself of the wire. I had just reached it when I heard the keeper's voice calling to mother wishing her good evening. I could see that mother and the keeper were engrossed in conversation back down the hedge some way, so without attracting any attention, I lay down at the side of the rabbit and with my back to the keeper. I killed the rabbit and covered it with grass to be collected later. I then distracted anyone's attention who may have been watching me, by jumping up and chasing a butterfly away out in the field. The conversation with the keeper ended with a cheerio, as he proceeded through the wood, having shared a little from the village of Sherborne where he lived. We had so few callers, that these short interludes with one of the other workers, allowed mother a little news from time to time.

Broadfield, like so many of the farms in this part of the Cotswolds, belonged to the Sherborne Estate, as did several villages. The estate covered many miles with the Stowell Park Estate bordering the western side, and it seemed that we were surrounded by wealthy landowners on all sides. I often wondered if any of them were aware of the amount of game there was on their lands. We certainly had a good supply at Broadfield, so the amount we had in our pantry from time to time, would not be missed.

I had learned so much in such a short time, regarding the ways of the countryside, and shared my knowledge with my sister Pat. She was a sturdy girl; she could run like a hare and was always ready to do her share of hard work, and was keen to share any adventure. My sister Peggy was a more gentle girl, and although she spent most of her time around the home, helping where she could, she was a great help watching over the three younger children.

The spring of 1931 came, and it was so nice to see the snow gradually disappear, we had to endure the dark and dismal days of rain, but in a few weeks we were to see the first snowdrops which told us that winter had really passed. One evening Pat and I made plans for our visit to the fowl house across the field. Then eventually the evening came; the weather was suitable as there was a light wind blowing away from the farm so we would be able to hear the movement of gates. It would also carry the aroma of the foreman's tobacco pipe to us; unlike the keeper's pipe which glowed red at times, the foreman's pipe had a metal cap, but the aroma could be carried quite a distance.

While the younger children were getting ready for bed, Pat and I suggested we carry more wood in for the fire. Mother must have thought we were in the shed cutting wood by candle-light, but we were on our way to another escapade. When our eyes had become accustomed to the dark, we moved off at a slow trot, the clouds were gradually moving away from the moon, and we were able to see much better. We moved around the outside of the large field, making sure we did not disturb the sheep as we moved fairly quickly towards our objective.

Eventually we came to the gate leading into the field where the fowl houses were; approaching the gate slowly in case either the keeper or foreman were there as they sometimes were, having a quiet smoke. But there was no one there, so we quietly climbed over the gate and left the shelter of the trees. We waited a few moments to listen for sounds of movement, my sister crouched a few yards away to keep watch, the light breeze would carry any sounds from the farm to her, and she would signal if she heard anything.

I quickly crept around the fowl house, to find that the door was padlocked, so I moved around to the flap at the side. I gently lifted the flap at the side. Having lifted the flap I had to signal Pat to come and hold it up while I bent down and quietly put my head inside. The birds were beginning to cluck, and move about on the perches, they had become aware of my presence. As my eyes became adjusted to the dark, I looked up into the gloom and saw the dark shape of a fowl. I had squeezed my shoulders inside by now, and I was aware that the wind had become stronger and that my sister was getting impatient by the tap I had from her toe. I said "damn" under my breath, grabbed the fowl's legs and neck and jerked it down, transferred both neck and legs to one hand while the other hand held the wings and I slid out on my stomach. Pat lowered the flap, and bending down low we made for the gate. The wind had become quite strong and would carry the sound, coming from the fowl house, away from the farm, so the farm dogs were unaware of anything. We were most grateful for the wind. Reaching the gate, we put our prize in a small sack we had for the purpose. I was conscious that I had a good deal of muck and feathers on me but they would be removed later. We hurriedly retraced our way around the field. We moved as quickly as possible past little groups of sheep, which ran for a short distance before returning to their grazing.

Taking a wider detour, in case we left a trail, we came to the wall bordering the field, this we would follow until we reached our cottage. Crouching under the wall we realized our captive was getting restless and it squawked once. So I decided to discourage it, this was achieved with a stone from the wall. I had located its head in the corner of the sack. I had laid over the sack until the death throes had eased, then we made our way home making sure no one saw or heard us enter the back-door.

Mother had eventually got the youngsters to bed, and was relieved when we crept through the back-door.

"And where do you think you have been?" she asked.

We said we had been for a walk, and found a chicken.

Her only response was to say, "You rascals, come on let's make up the fire, and we will get rid of the feathers."

Unfortunately we forgot that the draft carried some of the feathers up the chimney, and some were seen on the garden, but most of them had been blown out in to the fields and scattered well away from the house. No one seemed to notice them; but we had learned another lesson.

Needless to say the chicken was enjoyed by all — the bones were made in to a nice broth, and with many thanks and a "God forgive us for stealing", we made plans for another escapade. So whether by divine guidance, or sheer need for food our thoughts turned to pheasants, of which there was no shortage. We would enjoy the pheasant eggs in season, sometimes we would watch a hen pheasant return to her nest and settle on her eggs, then quickly creep up and grab the bird and return home with both bird and eggs. More often than not we would remove just two eggs every other day, from several nests, we knew the eggs were always fresh then. We also enjoyed eggs from moorhens, peewits, pigeons and mallards. We would not be able to have bacon with eggs, but several months of the year we were able to enjoy field mushrooms with the eggs. There were large quantities in our fields. No one else seemed to be interested in them. We also had a good supply of watercress in the brook. We kids had become quite good at foraging, and seldom went empty-handed.

The lighter evenings of spring encouraged us to think of the garden. So borrowing our neighbour's fork, I made some attempt to dig the garden, with mother's guidance. I planted some small potatoes we had saved for the purpose and hoped to have young potatoes and beef dripping one day. Our hopes did not rise to the roast beef or pork with lovely crackling, we had forgotten the flavour of such lovely meals, but at least we could dream of such things. Gradually colour began to come to the landscape and we saw Broadfield change from the cloak of autumn tints, when we arrived, and the barrenness of the fields with their stone walls through the winter which followed, and the snow which seemed to last for ever.

Now the days were getting longer, there would be much more work to do and times to play as well. Each day would bring a new adventure. We made friends with our neighbours. This was nice for mother, she often made an appearance at the front porch, and passed the time of day with one or another. We older children walked to school each day with the foreman's son Willy and daughter Alice. They were a little older than us, so we learned a lot with regard to school, and life on the farm. We learned what to do, and what not to do. This way we became friends with what local people there were —

these numbered sixteen in all. The Smiths would come up to Broadfield to play, or we would go down to Trowel Copse to see them. We had lots of fun, although I think we envied them, having a father to take care of them, and also bringing in a weekly wage.

CHAPTER 8

Father Returns

One Saturday, the weather being favourable, mother decided we should all walk into Northleach as she needed to see her mother. As usual we kept to the fields and would join the road at Lodge Park. I found myself as always, watching for anything that might present it self, and sure enough as I was walking near the wall surrounding the coppice, I saw a hen pheasant dusting herself on the back in the coppice. It crouched down in the leaves when it became aware of my presence, needless to say my second flint stone hit its head dead centre. I soon retrieved the bird, and hid it under my jersey. I was then able to give it to grandmother, hoping she would believe me when I said I had found it.

We were somewhat shy of meeting our old school friends; we were conscious of the clothes we had — we had out grown them, they had seen better days. In fact my short trousers were very short, which left skinny legs with wrinkled socks about half-way up my shins. My shoes had holes at the toes, they were the best I had, but seemed to be the fashion with many boys of my age. Of course, at home I had a pair of black plimsols with cardboard in to cover the holes in the bottom. On one occasion grandmother sent mother a bag of women's shoes from a Women's Institute sale; some were far too large for mother, but I was most lucky that there was a pair of high heel, lace-up, imitation crocodile leather.

I chopped the heels off, and found the shoes ideal for gardening. The girls seemed to be a little tidier than me; nevertheless we stayed inside granny's peeping through the lattice window at the passers-by, admiring the well-dressed and well-spoken ladies and gentlemen. The gentlemen would doff their hats when passing the ladies. According to granny, I would do the same when I grew up. But at present, my school cap was worn with the peak at the back. It was meant to stay on, even in bed at times when it was cold.

Mother enjoyed herself immensly, telling granny of all our experiences throughout the winter since leaving Northleach. It was the first long chat they had had, as there was little time for a long conversation normally when she was down to collect the 'parish relief' and do the shopping.

I had noticed that mother had taken the opportunity to write, and post a letter to father, while at granny's. We had heard fairly regularly from father, who said that he was hoping to apply to come home later in the year. Granny prepared tea for us and what a feast. Real bread and butter — such a nice change — the butter was called Sunny Pastures and had been purchased from Becketts the grocer where my cousin Carol worked. There was home-made jam, followed by some fresh Chelsea cakes from Spencers the baker, who had been a great friend. We would leave granny about four o'clock in the afternoon to make our way home, taking a few fancies with us. There was a long farmhouse loaf, and a small bottle of Camp coffee; a treat for father when he came home.

We had said our farewells to granny, and walked through the meadow field and climbed Mace Hill on the way home. From the top of the hill, we could look back over Northleach, which lay shimmering in the late afternoon sun. There was always a certain sadness in leaving; we all loved this conglomeration of stone houses and little cottages tucked in obscure corners, which made up this fine old market town.

Despite our sad memories and dislike for some individuals, as granny remarked one day, 'Northwich was a lovely garden, except for a few bitter weeds'. We hoped that one day our fortunes would change so that we too could have nice clothes and real shoes, posh shoes, like gentry — such as Mr Casssel, the butcher had, although we were grateful for the cast-offs we were given, and I am sure there were other boys and girls worse off than we were. Especially those who had the misfortune to dwell in the dark dismal streets of towns.

I thought how lucky we were to be free to live at Broadfield. I began to count up the good things we had — we kids had two secret camps; I had cut myself another stick, and recently made a catapult with some strong elastic granny gave me; and we were as free as the fresh air that blew over our fields. I expect those posh people we had seen in Northleach, had nice homes, but ours was nice and clean. We would wash the red brick floor if father was coming home, and put newspaper down to keep it clean. I remember mother called to us to ask us children to make haste, one of the girls said 'Yes, we'd better hurry in case robbers get in''.

It was so nice to turn our eyes homeward, and enjoy the beauty of the hedgerow and grass verges, the fresh air, the perfume of a freshly-mown clover field. We were able to look across the fields and see familiar land-marks, identifying our farm lands, as we called them.

Passing the village of Eastington down in the valley, we soon arrived at the high wall of Lodge Park where in the daylight everything looked serene and peaceful. We passed the large ash tree on the left which the man had hidden behind, as mentioned in a previous chapter. There was always a sense of foreboding when passing this part of our journey, especially at night. We hurried on home and were within sight of our turn off to Broadfield when a rabbit jumped out of the long grass and ran along the grass verge ahead of us.

Instinctively it was 'Tally-ho'. I gave chase with the girls running after me, and towards the high park wall which had partly collapsed. It was towards this mound of stones the rabbit scampered, to struggle through a hole so far up. I jumped up and made a grab for its back legs. In doing so I dislodged a stone with my shoulder and this set off the final collapse of the wall, which carried me to the ground. The result was a very bloody head. Of course we know that a little blood can make quite a mess, and mother wrapped my head up in a white pillowcase from the push-chair. Then she turned her attention to the younger girl, who had been screaming at the thought that I would lose my head. They were told by my sister Pat to be quiet as it could attract Billy the bull who was in the field opposite the park.

Too late, sure enough we heard his moaning as he left the cows to see what all the noise was. He was a bad tempered beast and inquisitive like most of his kind. His moaning turned to bellows as we hurried on. He arrived at the low stone wall and the single strand of barbed wire which was rusty and not very securely fixed to old wooden posts. Nevertheless, it seemed to deter him, and he followed us on his side of the wall. He would rise up over the wall and, with eyes rolling, he bellowed his challenge to all and sundry. We were pleased when we eventually passed an intervening wall which forced old Billy to stop. This did not please him one little bit and his bellows followed us until we had reached the lane leading to the cottages. On the rise we looked back to see him still watching us, although distance had somewhat deadened his bellows of frustration.

The only other time Billy chased us was one Saturday evening when my sister Pat and I went to meet father, when we expected him home for the weekend. Billy and his herd had been moved into what we knew as the bull field, which was at the bottom of the lane. Most of the walls in the adjacent fields had gaps in them and had no gates so that both cattle and sheep could range over many fields. By reconnoitring we could learn where the bull was and then take a path where he could not reach us. Nonetheless, we would take occasional sightings to make sure we had not been discovered by our arch enemy at the boundary wall. We sat near the roadside for possibly half an hour when we saw father appear in the distance.

We had lots to talk about and had forgotten about Billy the bull until we approached the head of the valley, where to our horror we saw Billy and his herd had moved from where we had seen them earlier and were clustered around the gate onto the road the other side of the valley. Father saw that both my sister Pat and I were rather scared, so he suggested we walk down into the valley out of sight of the herd where we could reach the road safely.

All was well and we were within a hundred yards of the wall, when to our dismay we heard Billy's bellow. Somehow or other he had heard us, and over the brow of the hill he came in full steam, and tail up; and that was when Pat and I reached the wall in record time. Only when we were safely on top of the wall did I turn to see where father was. To our dismay he had not followed us, but was walking directly towards Billy, who had stopped about a dozen paces from father. Here he stood head down, kicking the grass up with his front feet and mooing between bellows. He then began to prance up and down, and circled behind father. Father walked on, with Billy following groaning and blowing. This continued until father walked through the herd to the gate where we joined him to walk home as if nothing had happened. As for myself, I felt an utter fool being scared of such a beautiful beast, like Billy, 'blast his hide,' I thought. And here at twelve years of age I wondered if I would ever aspire to being a fearless man like my father. Yet here he was, walking up the lane, enjoying the prospect of being home with us for the weekend. We were so pleased, and despite his anger at times, we knew he loved us, and must have been terribly frustrated to have to work away. We longed for the day when he would return home for always. Mother needed his support so much.

Sunday evening once again arrived and father had to leave to catch his coach to London. As the evenings were getting lighter, Pat and I walked farther with him. Our farewells were moving to say the least. We would watch father out of sight, it was a long straight road, and he would turn to wave several times until as a mere dot in the distance he disappeared. We would then return home keeping to the road, and in the evening dusk, we would curse those who caused our family to be split up. We vowed that one day we would help mother and father make a fortune. We really did need more shoes, and we may then even afford a new coat for mother. Such were our thoughts.

It was now late spring 1932, and unknown to us, father had invited a friend of his from London. We came to know him as Uncle Harry.

He had been the purser on the passenger ship SS *Homeric*, and when next father came home, Uncle Harry came with him. He was awfully nice, and had lots of stories to tell us of his experiences at sea. During his stay, much was discussed in regard to the future, and on their way to London it was decided that father would apply to come home to stay.

This he did, and permission was eventually given. He was offered a job which was to be only temporary. At least we were at last all together. We often heard mother and father in conversation, and one evening we children were called in and mother said, ''Father and I have plans to start up in business again, but we need to keep it a secret for a while''. Father explained that he was in touch with a gentleman from Hull in Yorkshire. He would assist father in starting up a new fish business and would leave mother and father to arrange the best way to run the business from Broadfield.

Not everyone had heard that father had returned to stay, which was strange in a small and scattered community. I remembered one Saturday evening mother answered a knock on the front door to find one of the cottagers from across the fields who had presumed that mother was still alone. He proceeded to make references of our poor circumstances and laughed in her face. When she tried to push his foot from the door I could see mother was worried. I grabbed my nut stick and rushed out the back way to come up behind him. I then rushed into the front porch and raised my stick. I saw mother gently move to one side and there stood father who had arrived home through the back entrance.

''All right Bernie, I'll help the poor chap on his way,'' I heard, and saw a flurry of short blows to the man's face, which took the appearance of the bloody mess. When the man was allowed to rise up from the ground he was careful to watch father. He hastily walked backwards up the garden path, to retreat over the fields. I often wondered how he would explain his torn shirt and messy face to his family, but he must have given a lot of thought to his foolishness, because a few weeks later, while in Northleach, father met him and with a shameful face, he had the good grace to apologise to father and asked him to share a drink with him. Apparently everyone became friendly. It was then father began to give me lessons in boxing.

The plans for our future business went ahead. It was arranged for consignments of wet and dry fish packed in small wooden boxes containing ice which would arrive by train at Bourton-on-the-Water station twice a week. Transport for delivery was in the form of a tradesman's carrier bicycle. It had a large basket at the front and could carry nearly a hundredweight. There was a metal sign held between the framework which read "*Fresh Fish Daily. Fresh from the Sea*". This bicycle did sterling work covering a large area. Mondays and Tuesdays father would visit all the villages for orders, then deliver the fish on Wednesdays and Thursdays. Eventually the business required another pair of hands, so it was decided that as soon as I left school in the coming December I would help father.

At last Christmas 1933 came, I left school and borrowed a bicycle two days a week. I would cycle to Bourton, which was about six miles away, on Wednesdays and deliver orders in the village itself; then load up for my return journey via Northleach, where I would deliver my last orders of the day.

I would repeat the same journey on Thursday only to different customers. The remainder of the week I helped Bob Wilson, the farm manager. He was awfully nice to our family, in fact the Wilsons were all so very kind, and one could not have asked for better friends.

My first job on Saturdays was 'swede bashing' as we called it. This entailed the very cold job on a fresh frosty morning of lifting, topping and tailing the swedes, then collecting them in the cart, which was then driven to the swede pit under the hedge at one side of the field. Mangos were dealt with in the same way. Potatoes were in a separate clump nearby.

My favourite job was when Mr Wilson issued me with a satchel containing a pair of shears, some Jeyes fluid in a bottle, and a piece of rope. With my walking stick, a paper bag containing some bread and dripping, I would set off with precise instructions about treating sheep for maggots. My helpmate was a collie dog named Paws, he was nearly blind, but was a keen worker and a great pal.

First thing in the morning we would set off for the farthest fields, gathering the sheep into the corner of each field in turn. I would allow them to file past quietly, checking their rear ends for any sign of dirt, etc. Any needing attention were caught round the neck by my walking stick and turned quickly on to their sides, where I was able to cut away all mucky wool which often held flies' eggs or maggots. Diluted Jeyes fluid was used to disinfect the whole area. Sometimes it would take me three whole Saturdays to complete treatment of our sheep at Broadfield. We had three different flocks; Southdowns, Cheviots, and Kerry Hill, originally from Wales. In all we had just over two thousand.

I began to feel quite a man and quite grown up, especially when I was asked to help in the lambing pens. I was rewarded several times with lambs' tails, which made quite a tasty dish. I remember receiving my first shilling from Mr Wilson which I proudly gave to mother. Of course life was not all work. I spent much time during the evenings with Billy Wilson, or with my sisters. We had many happy times, such as when we lads blocked up the stream below Larkett Hill Wood. We lads soon stripped off and had a good soak in the lovely clear water. Then we would lay on the grass and dry ourselves. After we had left, the girls had fun splashing about. They had brought towels, unlike us lads who had not wanted to advertise our pool by carrying a towel.

I remember one evening when us kids had gone to bed, we heard father and Uncle Harry leave the house. I looked out my window to see father carrying a towel. It was not hard to guess where they were making for; a moonlight dip in our pool.

As children we, of course, had little idea of what the future held for us: life was still like a dream. But I'm sure the memory of those peaceful times at Broadfield would remain with us through life. If one awoke early in the morning, one would be greeted by the call of the curlew in the field next to our cottage. They seemed to give the signal to the other bird life, because from surrounding trees in the hedges nearby, and from the woods at Larkett Hill, the coppice at Trowel, came the morning chorus of blackbirds and thrushes, followed by the call of the wood-pigeons, and so many others. Their morning anthem to greet another day eventually reverberated over the whole area, and vibrated on one's eardrums, until as the sun became stronger their music lessened and they would return to the task of foraging for food in the hedge bottoms and fields. In my youthful mind, I was moved by this, and I looked forward to another day chorus as a Psalm of Praise, and the pigeon with its deep throated response as if it were the Amen.

Each season in its turn brought beautiful gifts, which helped to subsidise the 'parish relief' in the early days. Of course with father at home things would begin to improve. I still found time in the spring to search for the first blackbirds' nest. We knew where to find the mallards' nests also. There was one who would choose a nest site in a hole, half-way up a large willow tree. A little French owl had a nest in the same tree, which grew at the side of the stream in the valley. How lucky we were to be able to see and enjoy these things of nature. The whole place seemed to be festooned with colourful beauty wherever one looked. There were all the shades of greens and browns of woodlands; there were hedges covered in honey suckle, old man's beard, may blossom, all in their season. The quaker grass, ladies' smocks, scabious, hens and chickens; all names quite common to the Cotswolds, just to mention a few. The dogrose grew in great quantities all along the roadside. The hedges and verges held such a profusion of flowers.

The perfume was almost intoxicating in the late evening, and especially after a shower of rain. Bordering the stream below Larkett Wood, one could find reeds, rushes, catmint, sweet campion, wild forget-me-nots and cress when in season. We were to spend many hours along the banks, catching minnows, and often collecting frogs' spawn.

We had our own favourite hawthorn tree. When the fresh green leaves appeared we ate them and called them bread and cheese. These were followed by the plump red haws which we enjoyed.

There was an old garden to the west of Trowel Coppice where despite its neglect over the years, there were damsons, plum and apple trees. The gooseberry and blackcurrant bushes had masses of fruit but very small; nevertheless we were able to make good use of the fruit. There was an old stone cart hovel that we were able to explore, only to find a family of kittens resting in a heap of straw. As my sisters approached them, the mother cat left the hovel with a scream, the kittens scattered into the surrounding undergrowth, but not before my sisters had captured a lovely ginger kitten we were to call Sandy, and a black one naturally called Blackie. They became quite tame and joined our family.

In the summer months before father had been allowed home to stay, we children had played for long hours out in the fields. We looked after the younger ones, while mother concentrated on the housework. One of our favourite pastimes was showing the young ones how to make fairy houses. We would remove a stone from the garden wall, then using moss and grass, we would make a nest and put various birds eggs in. We would also collect beech nuts, crab-apples and hazel-nuts, which we would use for food, like the gnomes and pixies did — at least according to mother's stories. Who could deny that Broadfield was a place of dreams and imagination?

Of course, as I grew older, I wanted to spend more time with my two pals, Billy Wilson and Snowball Smith from Trowel Cottage.

As one can guess Broadfield would always remain a source of adventure and much enjoyment despite the trial and depredation of the early days. We felt free to enjoy this life of the countryside. In years to come we would most likely remember the happy times most. But I'm sure our experiences would help us in the days ahead, and there would be times when the memory of the peace and tranquillity we shared in the great open space of green fields with their interfacing stone walls, would return.

In the woods, hills and valleys with thick hedgrows, the only sound to be heard would be the hovering skylarks, the diving and looping peewits, the lambs bleating, and seldom a human voice. There would be the odd times when one could catch the voice of Charlie speaking to his horses out in the fields saying, "Get up Bess, ger out the furrow, steady, now, Ben, take it steady boy''.

There were times of laughter, sometimes tears, but I remember one occasion when we all had a laughing fit to bust our sides. Snowball Smith had spent a few days with his grandmother in Northleach. He had carried out several small jobs for her, such as running errands, chopping wood, etc., and was rewarded with a few coppers. As it was getting near November fifth, Guy Fawkes day, Snowball spent his three pence on fireworks instead of sweets, which he would often share with me. Little demon fireworks were commonly known as halfpenny bangers. On the Saturday morning Snowball hurried up to our house to show us his purchase, 'six little beauties' on which he had spent his three pence pocket-money. I must explain that Snowball collected his nickname due to his very blond, and almost white hair, which was close cropped except for a tuft that stood out just above his forehead. It was quite long enough for his mother to grab hold of if he misbehaved. He was quite tall and rather lanky for his age, and like myself seldom went anywhere without his old school cap on back to front. Our caps were acquired when we were about ten years old when the school decided we would have a uniform consisting of caps and blazers. Of course I must mention our blazers, which we held on to for a long time. These blazers were an emblem of education and were given when we had learned the times tables and could recite them like a chant from a Tibetan monastery. The pockets were now hanging off with sleeves which were now far too short, and were well greased due to us not having handkerchiefs. Nonetheless we usually kept the blazers for when we visited Northleach.

So it was that morning when Snowball presented himself at our house with a broad smile on his face. He beckoned me to follow him into the adjacent field, saying, ''Come on Bern, I've got sumthin' to show oo'', and proceeded to show us the bangers.

He then went on to explain that the boys in Northleach had found a way of throwing the firework without endangering their hands. He said you must have a hole in the toe-cap of your shoe like his, and just lodge the banger in the hole. When lit, and as soon as the firework began to fizz, one would flick one's foot and throw it away. ''I'll show you,'' said Snowball and promptly stuck a banger in the hole of his boot, igniting the touch paper with a match from an old tin he used for matches and dog-ends. He then stooped to blow the little red glow into life but the fizz came to life and Snowball began to flick his foot to dislodge the banger. But the movement caused the banger to slide farther into the boot and Snowball, his face getting redder by the second, and his blue eyes seemed to have grown in size, skipped and bellowed out a word of profanity that only terror would cause him to use, and with that the inevitable happened. Bang, and with a further yell Snowball danced over to a cattle trough and dropped his foot into the icy water. When he lifted his foot out it was to reveal the toe-cap of his boot open with his toes all black and bruised and very tender. The problem now was how was he going to get home and explain everything to his mother, who without a doubt would grab his little tuft of hair. I dread to think of the outcome, because boots were hard to come by. A good pair would have cost at least five shillings and eleven pence; and in those days a boot with a hole was better than no boot at all.

CHAPTER 9

Better Times

Father's business was progressing, so it was decided he should become more mobile. A motor bike and side-car should do very well. This would enable him to cover a large area in less time. An AJS motor bike, with sidecar, eventually arrived. In turn we were all treated to a ride.

The following day father drove in to see Granny Hyde. On arrival, granny's neighbour was heard to exclaim, "In heaven's name, what next? My how the Tingleys have come on."

Come on they certainly had, and thanks to God for his help in supplying our needs. Life indeed had improved, and I thought at the time how much better were our prospects for the coming Christmas, which was about a fortnight away.

It so happened that father and I were working in the town on Christmas Eve. By late afternoon we had finished deliveries, and were collecting outstanding monies. We then collected bread, groceries, and Christmas fare, and essentials such as candles, etc. Father gave me one shilling and sixpence to spend, and just before the shops closed at 9 o'clock p.m., I raced down to Eltom's grocery shops, where I was able to purchase eighteen oranges for a shilling, and a large bag of peanuts at three pence a pound. The girls would really enjoy them.

The motor bike and sidecar stood outside granny's, and it was duly loaded up by my father and I, including paraffin for a valor perfection stove with an oven that had been acquired recently. Mother would be able to roast our Christmas dinner. Father had purchased a large cockerel and it would last several days, which would be a great change from rabbit. Nevertheless we would take a rabbit when the chance came. Rabbit stew was a great meal when one was hungry.

Saying goodnight to granny, we pushed our conveyance on to the road, and father kicked it into life. The sidecar was full, so I rode on the pillion seat behind father; and off we went.

Unfortunately, as we turned into the road heading for home, the acetylene headlamp began to flicker and eventually became a tiny glimmer; then finally went out despite father's efforts to relight it. It would not work, so father said that if I would lay across the sidecar and hold a candle he had inside the headlamp glass we would then be able to continue. It was most awkward and I found it rather uncomfortable, especially when we began to chug off again. We had surmounted Mace Hill when the candle wax began to run over my fingers. This became more than I could bear and I said so to my father, who replied that never mind we are away from the town. So with a silent damn, I released the remainder of the candle. It was a moonlit night, the roads were quiet and there were no other travellers about. Father said that if we saw a light coming, we could stop and pretend to be broken down. We need not have worried because we saw no one. Even our local policeman must have been at home with his family.

We moved on in the bright moonlight homeward bound. There was a touch of frost in the air and swirls of mist were rising in the little valleys. It was a joy to have father home for Christmas. We had missed him the previous Christmas.

We spent most of the following winter evenings sitting around the fire in candle-light. We had a small lamp, but had to use the paraffin sparingly. It was so nice to have the family together, listening to father's account of his experiences in London, and the times he had spent in other countries during the Great War.

Mother had rescued father's medals when we were forced to leave the home at Northleach. I felt so proud to hold those medals, especially when father explained why he had received the Mons medal and bar, and how he came by the oak leaves attached to the other medals.

Father had also sent mother a piece of hessian material from a German spotter plane that came down near the front line in Flanders. On the hessian mother had embroidered the badge of the Medical Corps and flags representing the United Kingdom together with the message father had written. There was a wealth of stories that would become a source of interest and entertainment for many years.

The winter months found us more adaptable to country ways. With father to help us we were able to build up our stock of logs for the fire; but getting meat was still a job for Pat and I. One evening I went to meet the girls from school, and as usual Pat and I walked at the rear, keeping an eye on the younger ones in front of us. As we strolled along we noticed a man's bicycle leaning against the wall at the roadside. This was strange, we didn't recognise the machine, and so we thought we should try and see who it belonged to. Finding a suitable hiding-place in some bushes the opposite side of the road, we awaited events. It was as the sun sank, and wreathes of cold air began to rise over the valley that we saw a man appear from one of our fields bordering the spinney at the wash pool; a place where sheep dipping took place.

The man retrieved his bicycle and rode towards Northleach. Pat and I quickly left our concealment and followed the man's tracks back across the field down into the valley to find that our poacher had set snares far out in the field bordering the spinney. We realised he would come back in the morning to collect his catch and most likely sell the rabbits to his friends. This rather upset us because we always depended on the rabbits on our farm for the family. At least we decided to use this man's poaching to our advantage and let the snares remain, and told mother what we intended to do. Excitement kept us awake, but before the others were awake in the morning, Pat and I dressed and set off for the spinney across the fields, wondering what we would find moving across the fields. We came to the snares from inside the spinney and saw numerous rabbits jumping about in the snares. We observed this in the early morning light. There were one or two black rabbits which we ignored. With a swift blow with my stick we collected five rabbits, reset the snares, then made a swift retreat, hoping our tracks would not be seen by the poacher. He would come along about seven-thirty, so we hoped the frost and thick mist would cover our tracks. Pat and I carried our prizes home to find the others still in bed as it was Saturday morning and there was no school.

We had been angry to think someone was poaching on our land, but felt somehow rather pleased that due to him we were presented with five lovely rabbits, instead of having the task of chasing and catching them. We decided we would keep an eye on these snares, and the poacher, in case he moved them.

In the following spring we found a rabbit's nest in the grassy bank near the road. My eldest sister Peggy decided she would like one of the growing rabbits we found inside. The youngsters had their eyes open and were about a fortnight old. Peggy decided she would feed it with a doll's feeding bottle and cows' milk. It wasn't long before it began to chew young dandelions.

Our adopted offspring was called Binnie and became quite tame. It was a sweet little creature and would go for walks, or rather hops, while at the end of a lead. Father became rather fond of Binnie so he had the job of feeding her when Peggy was at school. All went well for several months, then early one morning one of the wild cats of the area happened to look through the window and saw Binnie on the carpet in front of the fire. This was too good to miss; there was the smashing of glass and the wild cat sprang through the broken window. The noise alerted father, who dashed downstairs; but not in time to save Binnie. It was over and the cat had hurriedly departed the way it came in.

The body of our little friend was buried later that day under the old apple tree, where most of our pets would eventually rest. We were to lose another pet in a different way. It was another rabbit; a lovely mother which had been given to me by my friend Snowball. It was already in kindle and had made her nest in the corner of our wood shed where they were quite safe from marauding wild cats. I had not told my family of the babies, in case my sisters came to investigate and disturb mother and babies, in which case she may have killed her little ones.

One evening, on returning home, father took me into the garden and with an apologetic look on his face he said, "I'm afraid I've had to kill your rabbit. You see Bern, it was suffering from a disease known as the mange. She had lost all her fur and I didn't want her to suffer. But don't worry, I will get you another one." I then realised father had never seen a milky doe as we called a rabbit with young. I proceeded to explain and I felt sorry for father who realised his sad mistake. I then had the painful task of killing the six-day-old baby rabbits. Fortunately they were still blind and knew nothing of life, and were too young to foster.

This little episode seemed to bring father and I closer together, and many times after this we would often take walks together. I remember confiding in him when I told him how I had stolen rabbits and pheasants while he was away, fully expecting to be reprimanded. But he said, "My son, I asked you to do your best for the family in my absence and you did. I'm sure he who sees all will understand. You are also becoming a great help to me. You must wait until we can afford a nice van for the business then we will get on, meanwhile we must have patience. You can still borrow our neighbour's bike and help me with deliveries." This meant a journey to Bourton-on-the-Water twice weekly, calling in on Northleach on the way home.

During one of our walks one summer evening, father and I had left the girls with mother to do some blackberrying, while we followed the hedge up to the larch wood called New Cover. As we drew nearer to the wood, father said, "If we crawl on hands and knees up to the corner, we shall see something I know you will like." So creeping on all fours we came to a position where we could look up the full length of the wood where we had a good clear view of a most wonderful sight. There was a vixen and four cubs — a grand picture to behold. As we lay there soaking in the beauty of everything around us, father said, "It certainly is a place of peace; a place where one can dream." Bird life was plentiful, there was hardly a hawthorn tree with its interlacing ivy that did not have a blackbird's nest. In some there were also pigeons and thrushes and the long hedgerows were favourite nesting sites for the yellow hammers, hedge sparrows, green finch, and warblers, just to mention a few.

In the large fields nearest our house, there were skylarks, and from dawn to dusk they hovered high above, filling the air with their lovely songs.

There were also peewits, and in the early morning we could hear the curlew in the cornfield. Both these birds were secretive with their nests; but with patience I was able to watch the birds alight and I was able to creep up to their nests to see the colour of the eggs which were camouflaged so well. One needed good eyes to see them.

One evening I heard mother and father in what seemed to be an important discussion. I felt sure something was afoot, and asked father what was wrong. Mother and father explained that they had thought that we should return to Northleach to live, as it would benefit us all, and would be nearer my father's area of business. There would be much better schooling for my brother and younger sisters. Mother dear, would find life a little easier in more modern accommodation. She would also be able to spend more time with granny.

I too, would find work and still be able to assist father. So plans went ahead, accommodation was eventually found, and once again Uncle Bob gave his services for the removal.

The morning came for the move, and once again mother sat up in front with Uncle Bob while we children walked behind the horse and cart. We cast many backward glances at the receding view of our beloved Broadfield, which had been our home, our refuge, the land of dreams. It all gradually disappeared from view behind the woods, to always remain a beautiful tapestry of colourful countryside in all its seasons, and memories of the experience of one family, that time would never change.

CHAPTER 10

Ups and Downs

Arriving at Northleach, we came to the house where we were expecting to rent rooms and had started to unload our belongings, when from a house opposite, we heard a shout. Turning to see who it was calling, we saw that it was the actual owner of the property, who with waving arms, emphasised the fact that we could not move into his property, and that his tenant had no right to sublet to us. This was a great disappointment to my mother, and she had no alternative but to apologise to the owner, in the absence of father, and ask Uncle Bob to once again store our goods in his sheds. This he did while mother took us children to Granny Hyde's.

That evening, when father came in from work, while having tea it was decided that he should take a room at the Red Lion public house, while mother and we children should stay with granny. It would be awfully crowded, but there was no alternative for the time being. The following week it was arranged that mother should take the children to an aunt's in Cheltenham until father could find accommodation locally. I was to stay with granny and try to find some work of sorts; jobs were scarce but I was able to help our neighbours with their gardens, and run errands.

A few weeks after, father managed to find rooms for the family in the area known as The Green just off the High Street; they soon settled in. My sisters Peggy and Pat, were invited to stay with Uncle Bob and Aunty Nell, and soon settled back in the local church school with all their young friends.

In the following summer father acquired a lovely little cottage known as Oak Cottage. It was a gable-fronted dwelling with wooden shutters which could be closed at dark. It was in the High Street a few doors from granny's, which was most convenient for mother. The place seemed to say 'welcome' the moment we stepped inside, and in very short time we had settled in. It was great to feel that this really was going to be our home for the future. An added joy, was that we were able to return to chapel life and join Sunday school again — something we had missed while at Broadfield.

My years at Broadfield had been spent mainly in the company of my sisters and little brother, and of course the Wilson and Smith families. But now I was able to meet many of my old school pals, although nothing would ever make me forget the lads out on the farm. Of course, having reached my teens, I found I was seeing Northleach in a different light; it was a new experience, everyone was becoming friendly and the old town itself was something I needed to explore all over again. I realized everyone was of course, four years older, but it was good to see that all our old friends had remained living in that quiet and gentle way of life they were accustomed to; and at this point I propose to mention one or two names that I feel are worthy of the name of friend.

There was our devoted Nurse Blackwell, who walked on her daily rounds. She was most kind to young and old alike — often over worked — that was when it was necessary to call on the services of Granny Hyde, who served as a midwife, and on many a night would sit at the bedside of the sick. She carried a bag, which contained white sheets and towels, which were used when bringing a soul into the world, and also to lay someone out for their departure. A remarkable woman was my gran.

Then there was Mr Spencer our baker who pushed his handcart round with the most lovely new bread and fancy cakes. And there was the humble Mr Hutt the dustman who helped to keep our waste paper and rubbish clear. They all went about their jobs with cheery smiles, and a tuneless whistle on their lips.

One of our dearest friends was the Revd Watkins of the Congregational Chapel which was to play such an important part in our lives. He was a keen Christian, and devoted to his flock, young and old alike. We were to remain friends for many years, even after we had all gone our separate ways. The memory of such people will always be with me.

I shall remember too, the pictures I shall always carry in my mind of the glorious sunrises, when the golden rays came up over the hill towards Burford in the east. It would bathe the town in its warmth through the day encouraging the ladies to come out on to their front steps to gossip a while, or to push the children up into one of the many lanes that could be found around the town; or they may have been content to stand and watch the odd motorised vehicle chug through the town — they were few and far between. I remember the occasion when a covered waggon, drawn by a pair of oxen came through Northleach advertising the product of OXO. Then there was the 'stop me and buy one' Eldorado ice-cream man on his tricycle, who drew the children to spend their ha'pennies on the fruit sticks. By this time the sun had run its course. The children had returned from the meadow where they had played beside the stream most of the day, and the sun, a huge red ball sending coloured rays the length of the whole town, sank gradually down over the hill towards Cheltenham in the west. The shadows would gently form, and often a mist would rise in the meadows where the children had played earlier. The last songs of a thrush would be heard in the large ash tree that stood at the end of the lane joining the meadow.

It had been a long hard day for those lucky enough to have a job. To be employed was most fortunate in those days; but this did not prevent the men from finding time to go into their gardens in the evening where they would work until almost dark, until time for supper, leaving behind them little fires of grass, weeds and leaves, with little spirals of smoke rising up in the evening sky to float over the meadow. The pleasant odour of burning squitch, almost like incense, was most pleasant to one such as me, who loved the sights, sounds and smells of the countryside, and things that were a part of one's youth.

I was enjoying this life in Northleach, but I was becoming conscious of the fact that I ought to find regular employment, so that I could earn some extra money to help support the family — at least I felt that I would like to purchase my own clothes. I was still helping father two days a week. I received my food, but I longed to have my own pocket-money. I remember receiving two shillings and sixpence (half a crown) one day as I had terrible tooth-ache, and was told to run down to the visiting dentist, who held a surgery in Gardner's paper shop. I needed no urging to get help for the pain which was almost blinding me, so I hurried through the shop to the sitting-room. Here I met Mr Alcorn in his white coat and proceeded to tell him of my problem and could he please help me as he had helped my mother years before when he took all mother's out at one sitting. I had completed the story of my life and stopped for breath, that was when he seemed to prick my mouth with something. I didn't see what, but as my eyes were tightly shut, they seemed to want to remain that way. When I did manage to peep a little it was to see the dentist advancing from the table with his hands held behind him. He leaned forward smiling and said, "Right sonny, let's get rid of that nasty tooth. Open your mouth just a little. There let's press it down a bit," and then 'hey presto,' I felt my body rise like an arch in the armchair, and then as I settled down I slowly opened my eyes to see the dentist holding the tooth in his hand. Glory be! "That's it sonny. Put your money on the table," he said. "That tooth will give you no more trouble."

I remember Uncle Bob inquiring if I would care to help him in his keepering job. I jumped at the chance of doing anything to bring a little cash my way. He asked me to meet him early on the Saturday morning. This I did. He supplied me with a bicycle and a stick with which I would beat the woods for pheasants. This was to be my first experience of beating for game. I did not like the idea of driving the pheasants out to the waiting guns, but I soon overcame this feeling when I realised that the birds were bred for food, and I had had my share of birds in the past. It was a long day, but I went home with a rabbit for granny, and half a crown for mother. Not bad for one day's work.

On one occasion it rained most of the day, and the first drive after lunch, included driving the birds out of a field of kale. The kale grew so tall it came up to my waist. Naturally I was wet to the skin before I had completed the drive, but as I proceeded through the field in the driving rain, I noticed a covey of partridges rise up and fly towards the main road where they rose up to clear the telegraph wires, and I noticed that the wind drove the birds into the wires. After completing the day's work, I followed the road to the spot and found to my delight, three plump little bodies, which I promptly popped into my inside pockets. Granny was pleased, as partridge was a tasty meal.

On shooting days, we would often stop near a farmyard for lunch and gather round in a cart hovel if it were raining, or outside on the straw bales. Sometimes the frost or thick fog would keep us stamping our feet to keep warm. The under-keeper would lay a large piece of sacking on the ground on to which he would tip a dozen or so cottage loaves, which he would break in half, then add a pile of pieces of Cheddar cheese — each piece was as much as mother would buy for a whole week — so if there were any to spare, I took some home for the family. As I did not like the beer they supplied, I would take a bottle of cold tea.

I had been tempted to try smoking a cigarette like one of my pals, so having saved threepence, I purchased a tuppenny packet of Woodbines and a penny box of Ship matches. I took them with me on the next day's shooting. I was stood in a quiet corner of a coppice, and decided it was the ideal spot to try a cigarette. So I lit up and thought that I must have looked a right charlie, with fag in mouth. Every now and then I would cough and splutter, while thrashing my arms and stamping my feet to keep warm on such a cold morning with thick mist swirling around. Eventually, I decided smoking was not for me, and besides I had promised granny that I would not waste my pocket-money on such things. My next problem was to get rid of the smell of smoke that clung to my hair and clothes. But I need not have worried, by the end of the day I had been through farmyards, and smelt of everything but smoke.

I remember going to help one farmer thrash his corn ricks, and my job was to remove all the waste chaff from under the drum. When at the end of the day I still had a large heap of chaff to take to a shed for bedding. The other workers had finished and been paid off; but the farmer waited until I had cleared everything, then walking up to me, he said, "Now my lad, here's your money, you've earned it. Remember to do your job to the best of your ability, you will then have the respect of the person that employs you. You will never regret it."

Soon after this I heard that the contractors building the aerodrome at Little Rissington a few miles up the road, were in need of workers. I went to see the general foreman who was lodging in Northleach. I was offered a job as carpenter's mate, at sixpence an hour. A bus collected workers from Northleach at 6.30 a.m. six days a week. I enjoyed working with the carpenter who was most capable at his craft. I had much to thank him for, and made good use of the knowledge and experience later in life.

The whistle went at six o'clock at the end of the day. We were home by 6.30 p.m. This allowed me time to do an odd job at home, and possibly a game of cricket or football.

Towards the end of the year, father purchased a Morris van for his business. He needed another pair of hands, as trade had increased. So it was decided I would join him. Both mother and father were keen to progress; so through the day father and I would be round the villages, and in the evening we would do another delivery of 'hot faggots and peas'; they were long days, but rewarding.

Of course it was thanks to my cousin Harold, who had taught me to drive a vehicle, in the first instance. But father had a licence, and would drive in and around the town. It was necessary for me to have a provisional licence — this had recently become law. I think I was the only person to hold one at the time, so few had the opportunity to take up driving.

Unfortunately, the following year, returning home one evening, some cattle ran amok. We thought that perhaps our headlights had startled them. They burst through a fence and jumped from the high bank, one beast landing on the bonnet of our van, to slither off into the road where it lay thrashing its hind legs; the front legs appeared to be broken. I remained there while father went to notify the farmer, who quickly came and put the poor beast out of its misery with an axe. This unfortunate accident put father and I out of business for awhile. Someone heard of our plight and said that there was no need to be without work and gave both father and I a job with the Ministry of Transport, doing a traffic census on the main Cheltenham to Oxford road. Father did from 7.30 a.m. to 7.30 p.m. I carried on through the night. We had a small hut for shelter, and a fire brazier for warmth, as it became quite cold through the night. Sometimes large lorries came by, but usually it was motor cars. I was always alert with my torch so I could count the wheels of each vehicle as it passed. Sometimes I heard the scuffling of feet and an old tramp would come into the light of my fire. He would leave his perambulator on the road and draw up to the fire to warm his hands. Then he would ask if he could boil his billy can. Sometimes I gave them a slice of my bread which they would promptly toast on the fire. It was quite nice to have someone to chat to for an hour or so. Some of the tramps I met were so well spoken. I would wonder what had caused them to take to the road. It was quite possible that they too had lost everything like my parents.

This work was completed in the fortnight. Father remained with the ministry, while I was asked to assist an elderly lady who lived at the Manor in the High Street. She had a small retail milk business to supplement her living, and she needed someone to help. I would start at 6 a.m. and meet her crippled son who would drive his motor bike and side-car to collect a churn of milk from a farm some miles out. On his return we would carry the churn into the dairy where I would bottle and cap the bottles; after which I would help deliver the milk round the town. The son who owned the Union Hotel in The Square gave me several jobs to do after I had dashed home to have my breakfast at 8.30 a.m. There was always the job of filling up the various fixtures in the bar with bottles from the cellar, and wood and coal to be loaded into the hearth in the lounge. At half-past ten I would return to the Manor where there would be a list of jobs to do through the day. At 11 o'clock, I would find a glass of milk and a piece of cake for my lunch on the seat in the back porch. After this I would do the various tasks awaiting me, such as window cleaning, feeding the chickens, collecting eggs and vegetables from the garden. I would shut the chickens in for the night at dusk, and on the stroke of 6 p.m. I would call out goodnight to the lady of the Manor and make my way home. It was a sixty-two hour week. I was paid the huge sum of six shillings and sixpence, a week. I was able to give mother six shillings — this left me with the odd sixpence. I would spend two pence on my weekly book *The Cage-birds Weekly*; two pence on a quarter of Golden Charm toffees; and two pence for the chapel collection; and I was quite happy with my lot, and proud to be able to help mother at the same time.

Unfortunately my new-found wealth did not last very long. My dear old employer fell ill and was unable to carry on with the business. The milk round was closed down, and once again I was looking for a job. My eldest sister Peggy was doing a part time job at the hairdressers. Sister Pat, a member of the local Girl Guides, was found a position as nanny to the children of a local farmer. The guide mistress was a relation to the farmer and recommended Pat for the job. So the girls were doing their bit to help with the family expenses. But there was little I could do to help until something turned up.

My next job came quite unexpectedly after the evening chapel service. The gentleman who played the organ was an old friend of the family of long standing. He asked me to call and see him the following morning. This I did, and was so surprised to be asked if I would like to work for him. The job would entail odd jobs around his drapery shop; a little gardening; and driving my employer round the villages, selling ladies' and gents' clothes. Naturally I accepted, and arranged to start the following Monday morning. I had passed my driving test in Gloucester at the first attempt, and settled into a most satisfying occupation. Fridays and Saturdays were spent in the shop behind the counter from 8.45 a.m. until 9 p.m.

Taking me to one side one Saturday evening, my employer said it was nice to have a chapel lad in the business, and he would like me to dress a little smarter for some one in my position. Would I therefore ask mother if she would permit me to purchase the necessary clothes. Mother agreed to this of course, and I was duly measured up for a grey pin-stripe suit, costing the incredible sum of thirty-two shillings and sixpence; a white shirt, three shillings and eleven pence; one pair of black shoes at five shillings and eleven pence three farthings; one pair of black socks one shilling and five pence three farthings. I was asked to pay two shillings and sixpence per week.

At last I was able to give mother one pound per week as my wage was one pound ten shillings. My only other expense was the stoppages for the insurance and employment stamp, which was five pence and seven pence respectively. I could hold my head up high. I felt quite respectable — a wonderful job and I could save four shillings a week with ease. I had so much to be grateful for — life had a new meaning. I even learned to thank God for my new-found wealth, at the same time asking his forgiveness for my misdeeds as a child, and those days when I could not miss the opportunity of pinching a rabbit or such, but thank God those days were passed.

My half-day was on a Thursday. This allowed me to walk Pat back to the farm for six o'clock in time to help the cook prepare the evening meal for the master and mistress of the house. Apparently once the children were in bed, Pat's duties turned to the kitchen, and after this she was given the ironing and sewing until ten p.m. Her day started at five-thirty a.m., so I could quite understand when she said that she intended to look for another job. She was a keen worker, but did not like being used like a slave.

A few months after, a job as a voluntary aid assistant was vacant at the old workhouse, which was being turned into a cottage hospital. Pat soon settled in and became quite a proficient nurse. Around about this time I joined the St. John Ambulance Brigade, and took up voluntary ambulance work in the district. I passed my first-aid certificate prior to this, and was tempted to join my pals who were all joining the Territorial Army, but my father had said that as I was already doing medical work, it would be advisable to join the Military Hospital Reserve; in the event of war I would be of more help to the wounded. He was speaking from personal experience because he had joined the army at an early age. By putting his age on, he became a regular soldier at sixteen, serving in various parts of the Far East, then to return in time to join the British Expeditionary Force to go to France in 1914, serving in the trenches for six years. He eventually came home safely, a fully qualified medical man, but also a huge store of knowledge, much of which he was able to share with me. Not even mother knew that I had volunteered for the Royal Army Medical Corps, and I was often taken to task by my Uncle Bob, and others, for not going to the training weekends on Salisbury Plain with my school pals.

In 1938, the news was very unsettling from the Continent. The Nazis were on the move, our roads from London were busy with evacuees — quite a large number came to Northleach. Everyone will remember how Chamberlain came back from Munich, with the promise of peace in our time. Slowly people began to filter back up the motorways to London, several remained in Northleach, where they had settled in with jobs, homes and schools, and they were reluctant to leave the peaceful atmosphere of our old town.

Two friends of ours, Reggie Bowers and Gladys Cripps, returned to London in the summer of 1939, but sadly Gladys was killed in one of the first air raids on the city the following Christmas.

I remember thinking how terrible it was to think that our country was actually at war. What did the future hold for us? I would have been rather awestruck if I had known what the following seven years were going to be like for me.

With these thoughts clouding my mind, like many more people I would try not to look too far ahead. I was inclined to think of the past, call it sentimentality if you will, at least it brought back happy memories — indelible pictures of my early youth — and sweet is the memory of the little groups of youngsters singing carols in the streets at Christmas. I remember two little girls that came to Granny Hyde's door and timidly tried to sing the old favourite carol, *Away in a manger, no crib for a bed.* The kids would receive the few coppers after singing four lines then move on; apparently they had nothing else to offer. My two sisters joined their two friends Molly and Ena, and being older they would sing several carols, such as —

Like silver lamps in the distance shine, the stars are sparkling bright,
The bells of the city of God ring out for the Son of Mary was born tonight,
The night is past, and the dawn at last, is coming with orient light.

After a couple of hours out in the frosty night air, the girls would return to our home with cold hands and faces. With bright rosy cheeks, they would come into the living-room, where the money they had collected would be equally divided, and used to make their Christmas a little more festive. We lads, being more venturesome, would visit some of the larger houses in the town on Christmas Eve, with some success; but a group of young men, some belonged to the church choir, formed quite a sizeable party and really went to town — they had someone to play a concertina, to add to the tone of their carols. They also had several lanterns on poles with candles in. This all went to add to the Christmas spirit as they went from street to street. They would make a stop at the Sherborne Arms pub for a little light refreshment. After a couple of carols, there would be a short walk to the Red Lion, where another oiling of the vocal cords would take place. The party would then move on to the country houses, and more often than not find their way to the Manor at Leygore about three miles out of Northleach. The village of Turkdean had received a programme of festive songs on the way. Now it was the squire's turn. This was to be the final venue for the night, and as was customary, the squire and his wife were there to greet the choir. They would all gather in the main entrance hall, with its holly and ivy and gay decorations hanging from the ceiling, while a huge log fire burned in the stone fireplace. The staff had also come to join in the singing in true Christmas spirit. After singing one or two carols requested by the lady of the house, the squire suggested refreshments could be served. The cook/housekeeper carried in a large bowl of hot punch, and a maid brought in a huge tray of hot mince pies to round off the evening. After a couple of verses of *We wish you a merry Christmas and a happy new year*, the lads began to replace their coats and scarves, and on reaching the front steps turned to call 'A Happy Christmas to you all'. Replacing their hats, they made for the road that led to Northleach and home, carrying with them the collecting box which had become considerable heavier. They had a comfortable warmth in their tummies thanks to the hot punch they had drunk amongst other things during the evening. It was only when the party had gone some distance that it was found that one of our number was missing. No one had seen him since leaving Northleach. One chap remarked that the fellow seemed to be well lubricated at the Red Lion pub. One was heard to remark, "Never mind, he'll turn up, I dare say."

They were well on the way, when in the distance up ahead, could be heard a voice endeavouring to reach the top notes of "Noel", and as they approached the spot where the lone singer was doing his best to entertain, they saw that it was their missing member, well and truly filled with local brew and possibly home-made wine. There he was standing in bright moonlight, beating his arms, not in time with his rendering, not to a cottage as he imagined, but to a hay stack just inside the field, it made a most amusing picture to say the least. It took several minutes to persuade the chap it was time to go home. In the process of helping him over the gate, he fell to the hard frosty ground, and despite efforts on everyone's part, our vocalist would simply not stay on his feet, in the end it was decided that two chaps would hasten to Northleach for some sort of transport. It was no joy waiting about for almost an hour in the cold and frosty night. Eventually the lads turned up with the only transport they could borrow, it was the local roadman's wheelbarrow. After many grunts and groans on the part of our would-be chorister, he was eventually loaded, and taking it in turns he was delivered to his own doorstep. Strange to say it was his father's house, and he was the road sweeper. It certainly caused quite a laugh in the following days.

I would carry memories of such times as this in the years ahead, and would remember with great affection a picture of my wonderful Gloucestershire pals, kindly folk, with their ready smile and word of greeting.

The voice of one such friend with his wonderful brogue, comes to me. His name was Alfie, his nickname was Dreamer, and on Saturday evenings, after work on the farm he would call in to my cousin Harold's fish and chip shop to collect something for his tea, and as usual this is what transpired:

Alfie. Wup Drib (Drib being Harold's nickname, short for dribble, due to his ability to dribble at football).

Harold. Wot O, Dreamer ow bist? Nuther nice day?

Alfie. Ah, 'tis Drib?

Harold. Wots swant Dreamer? Sunthin fer tea?

Alfie. Yea plis Drib? Same as I alus as? A fish and a penuth.

Harold. Yew be all togged up Dreamer? Asent bin to work today?

Alfie. Corse I haeve, but I bin on muck cyart aw dey? I ummed so I washed, and togged?

Harold. I someow thought thee wert agoin some wer.

Alfie. No I baint agoin eny wer? Well not special like. Der sey I'll caw in tu Red Lion on wey wum.

It was no surprise to me to hear my sisters telling mother some of the things they had heard the locals say, and were inclined to speak with the same sort of brogue. They, like myself, had become a part of these lovely Cotswolds. It was good to see my young brother take his place with the family in chapel on Sundays, and to have made so many friends. Life was indeed colourful and peaceful in our old town.

I had noticed that my sisters and brother had taken to helping the neighbours with odd jobs. The elderly folk seemed to enjoy having them call. I remember times calling at granny's possibly just before a mealtime and she would say "Well. Come on, draw up. Help yerself ter greenstuff, the bito meat cost I nine punce."

I remember a local character whose nickname was Dubby. He would roam the countryside and seldom returned home without a rabbit or a bunch of watercress. He knew that granny was always a good customer, and on knocking at gran's door the interchange was something like this.

Dubby. Lo Missus Ide? Swant a rabbit or somr watercress?
Granny. Ah that I do Dubby. Werst get they frum then?
Dubby. I fund 'em in meadow at Yesinton (Eastington) tha snow.
Granny. Well dun Dubby. Thanks, now owbe yer keepin these deys?
Dubby. O' oi be pretty well missus. Ow'be yer legs now? Ast thee still got that ther arteritus? Cor ow thee dust manige, I dunt nowe? Ah well missus. God help ee? Cheerio.

The 'haitches' were dropped in most cases, in the real Gloucestershire dialect, but this did not detract anything from the honesty and beauty that surrounded the lives of my Cotswold friends. My sister Peggy was a keen flower grower; in fact I called her my flower girl, due to her fondness of flowers. Some of her favourites were love-in-the-mist, and nasturtiums, also tall 'olly-yawks' as she called the hollyhocks.

When she was recovering from an illness once, I would take her on long walks. We would pass the sweet shop on the way, where I would purchase a tuppenny bar of Cadbury's chocolate. The eight squares would be chopped in to sixteen bits of chocolate and was made to last until we got home for tea.

Our conversations were mainly about the future — we would endeavour to have elocution lessons as we walked along, including 'haitches', just in case we should meet one of the opposite sex, whom we may wish to impress. Cor just fink uv it? But imagination and dreams had been, and still were, a part of our lives.

The summer of 1939 had been remarkably warm and peaceful in our old town; Uncle Bob said it was the peace before the storm. Father said the storm clouds were gathering in Europe, but mother said keep hoping and praying, and in her wisdom said "No matter what happens my son, if you do have to leave us, please remember the things your father and I have taught you. Don't forget the life you lead and the duties you have to fulfil will build your character for your future life.''

Our minister at our chapel, when wishing me Godspeed, gave me a small card on which was written the following words. *I know whom I have believed, and am persuaded that He is able to keep that which I've committed, unto Him against that day.*

CHAPTER 11

A New Life

On Sunday September 3rd, I was greeted with the news that war had been declared. I had been to chapel and had walked up the street in time for lunch to find my family awfully upset, speculating on all the possibilities of invasion, and if I would really have to go to war.

My pals moved out the following weekend to join the British Expeditionary Force in France — I was reminded by one person that I ought to have been with my pals — but my father and I knew that our plans were best, and at seven-thirty in the morning, on Tuesday October the 3rd, there was a knock at the door and our St. John Ambulance Superintendent said I had to report to Crookham Camp, Aldershot, that day; and accompanied by three other lads, off we went. Catching a train at Cheltenham we arrived eventually in Aldershot and the camp by four-thirty (p.m.).

One of the lads who travelled with me, was the son of the head gamekeeper on the estate where we had spent many happy days beating for the guns. Not having been away from home before, I decided to remain close to him, as he was older and more experienced in the world. So Bill and I palled up, and that evening we transferred from the reserve into the regular army for the duration of hostilities. At two bob a day we would not save a fortune, but we had volunteered. We were issued with an army number, mine was 7519501, one blanket, one tin plate and a tin bowl which was used for several purposes other than tea, and speaking of tea — one remembers our first meal in the army, which happened to be tea, dinner and supper all in one.

My parents would have looked on with horror as we lads filed into a long wooden hut, and sat either side of trestle-tables looking forward to our meal as we had not had a meal since breakfast at home in the morning. It was not long before our dreams of a nice roast beef dinner, followed by a nice steamed pudding vanished completely as a cook arrived with a huge tray stacked with slices of bread and margarine — the tray came to the head of our table and the bread sliced two at a time were slid along the table collecting dust and grime on the way; fortunately it was only the bottom slice that was uneatable; there was no etiquette at table, a large metal bowl containing boiled eggs followed the way of the bread, but thanks to their shells were eatable and enjoyed. Our basins came into use when large buckets of strong sweet tea were supplied. Everything we saw or used could well have been equipment stored after the 1914-1918 war, then again, there was a war on, as we were reminded from time to time. After this meal we were dismissed and allowed to use the remainder of the evening settling into our quarters, a wooden hut with a round stove in the middle, its round chimney going through a hole in the roof. The hut held thirty-two men. A small room at the end was for the sergeant who became our sergeant-major within two days of our arrival. It was advisable for two persons to sleep together, this allowed us to sleep on one blanket with one to cover us; of course we slept in our clothes, just taking our jackets off; but soon to be donned again when the temperature really dropped.

It was a terribly cold night with a thick blanket of fog — which seemed to creep into the hut from under the door or through the loose windows — despite our efforts to stop this by pushing newspapers into gaps around the windows. Just before midnight, one chap was so fed up he said he would light the stove. Some of us who had not been able to sleep rose up, and as no fuel had been supplied, we broke up wooden rifle racks around the hut to make the fire. Outside it had begun to snow.

Reveille was at 6 a.m. — the first bugle call of the day. Roll-call was to be at 7 o'clock. Folding our blankets, we then turned to the problem of having a wash and shave. This was to be quite an exercise — the showers were in a tin shed; there was no light, or bowls, so it was a matter of turning the shower on a little to allow water to drip onto your shaving brush. Of course holding the brush up high enough to catch the water meant that the water would run down your arm and trickle down your clothes — in the gloom one could just identify other bodies moving about. Noticeably there were exclamations when one turned on a tap too much, this was followed by typical army language; no place for a chapel lad believe me. Nevertheless, I was to become very fond of these men, and share their privations in the years to follow.

After roll-call, we went back to our canteen hut and once again were given bread and marg and boiled eggs — I'm sure the cook could have done better — but rations were short, as was most everything. We had a parade around 9 a.m. and found that huge numbers of men had answered the call to service, out of the St. John Ambulance and British Red Cross, all volunteers and reservists like myself. An officer with a sergeant-major counted the number of men, and split the whole parade into units of one hundred and twenty men.

My unit became the 1st Light Field Ambulance, and we marched off to have a medical check. While there, we had an inoculation of T.A.B. and this was followed by a vaccination; we returned to stand in parade until the last man came out adjusting his clothes — the snow had almost gone although it still threatened. At ease, we were able to stamp our feet and then had orders to file into another hut, here we found the dentist. I had nothing by way of treatment, but poor Bill came out spitting blood; he was to have the remainder out in a week, and would have false teeth.

That evening, Bill and I went to the local pub where he indulged in a double whisky and I had a very large lemonade — nice at the time, but what would my grandmother have said!?

Rations were still rather short after a week and we also had not been kitted out — we were still in civies and looked a sorry sight I am sure, doing our drills and exercises on Tweedledown Racecourse adjacent to the camp. My brown shoes were going down at the heel, and my brown pin-stripe suit was mud spattered and crinkled at the knees. This suit had been given to me by my cousin Harold and still smelt of fish and chips; it caused quite a laugh in our barrack room. One lad went up to my jacket hanging above my kit, and closing his eyes while sniffing at the coat said, "I'll have mine with salt and vinegar". These lads were the greatest, and now that the unit had been formed, started training in earnest — in the second week our kits had arrived including a groundsheet and an extra blanket — for which we were eternally grateful.

Our route marches were good, despite sore ankles and blistered feet. One lad was prepared for this and had brought a huge tin of lanolin; we were so grateful to him. Medical training was at the Cambridge Hospital in Aldershot and for some weeks we spent most of our days studying.

On December 8th we moved out in army lorries up into Hertfordshire where field training took place. I was to be a stretcher-bearer until I passed my first examination. We were billeted in private houses in the town of Knebworth — I was able to write home at this time; and as we had Sundays free, and I was able to make my letters interesting without infringing the security rules. Life was certainly full of excitement to a lad such as I, who had been very much the homely type. Never mind said I, it was all a part of my desire to become a good medic first and a soldier second.

At Christmas the married men were allowed home, but we faired fairly well ourselves; we took over a school as a dining-hall and sat for a very good Christmas dinner with the traditional turkey and plum pudding. The colonel and junior officers did the carving and serving, and for a brief hour or two one almost forgot the reason for being there at all. As I left the school hall and walked down the street, a lady and gentleman stopped me and asked if I would care to go into their home for Christmas tea. This was absolutely wonderful, I walked into a warm hallway where I hung my army greatcoat, helmet and gas mask, then followed these kind folk into a cosy sitting-room. The gentleman and I found plenty to talk about, and the lady of the house quietly went about preparing tea.

We enjoyed a very pleasant evening together and I promised to call again. I once again donned my coat and made my way back to the house, where due to having no lights at all in the billets, I spread my blankets on the palliasse on the floor and lay there in the dark wondering what my family were doing at home. And, I found, over the years in some of the most unsavoury places and difficult circumstances I more often than not would find myself thinking of the dear ones I had left behind and remembered them in my prayers wondering what the next day would bring.

There was still lots of ice and snow about when we moved off again and marched into Wiltshire a few miles from Salisbury. We were once again in private accommodation with families who were asked to supply a bed and a bath when convenient. The family I was fortunate enough to be billeted with, were so homely and awfully kind; they had a son and daughter which added to the happy atmosphere. Another medic joined me at Spring Cottage — his name was Basil and was such a good chap — and was a source of inspiration to me; and through his encouragement I was able to sit and pass my second class nursing examination.

Our time here in the village of Redlynch came to an end in March and we moved to Southampton where we sailed for France and the British Expeditionary Force. We landed at Cherbourg and marched from the boat to where our lorries and ambulances were parked. We had a brief meal then moved off to the main forces which at this time were on the Belgian frontiers. Most of April was spent near Paris but in May we gradually moved northwards and remained near a town called Lille then Aberville; we seemed to move every other day.

German planes had been seen from time to time but everything seemed quiet in our area until we heard what seemed to be thunder in the distance. We were soon to realise that this drumming of sound came from the Belgian frontier area. Soon news came through that the enemy had broken through and was marching into France. We moved on the morning of May 19th northwards and camped at a farmyard, the ambulances and lorries were hidden under the apple trees in the orchard; we medics slept in the loft of the barn, which was reached by stone steps on the outside. The farmer was most kind, he would bring us buckets of cider round in the evening. He was a very elderly man and apparently had lived there in the previous war. He stood looking towards the front one evening and remarked that the British would drive the Hun back into Germany — we hoped this was so, but the sounds coming to us seemed to be getting closer and I noticed the colonel had sent a dispatch rider off in a hurry somewhere — we had no wireless in those days so we had to rely on the dispatch riders so very much, who did a marvellous job.

As the evening drew on, and we sat around our vehicles, there seemed to be an air of expectancy despite the jokes and small talk among the chaps. I suppose the knowledge that no news had come through while there was so much activity a few miles away, that to us, who had had little experience if any, of war and its noise, and the clamour of moving tanks, filled us all with trepidation as we began to realise that on the morrow we may find ourselves doing the very work we had been trained for. I remember wondering if it would be anything like the war my father had experienced.

In the late evening, as there were no orders to move, we chaps climbed up the stone steps into the hay loft and simply lay on the hay just removing our steel helmets and went to sleep. In the early hours of the morning, somewhere around 2 a.m., one of our night picket came hurriedly up the steps, woke us, and said we were to make for the vehicles quickly and quietly as the enemy had broken through and were spreading out northwards. We fumbled our way through the orchard and mounted up. Our unit moved out into the lane leading to the main road some hundred yards away. Once in the lane we halted and waited for the signal to move ahead — no lights were allowed, so it was rather miserable waiting in the cold air of the early morning. We had been there about half an hour when German Stukas roared in from the east, bombing an area about half a mile away.

It was at this point that my pal Bill swore and said that he had left his false teeth up in the loft. It was his habit to take his teeth out, wrap them in his handkerchief, and normally put them in his pocket; but on this occasion he had put them on the wooden beam just above where he was sleeping. In his haste he had forgotten them. So it was any volunteers to retrieve them? Anyway, he was my pal, and I said I would creep back to the loft. As we came to this decision, the sergeant-major came along to tell us that a column of Germans were coming along the main road, and we were to start the engines and be prepared to make a speedy retreat. Anyway without thinking of the possibilities, we climbed out of the lorry and dashed back to the farm, doubled over to keep in the shadows. Fortunately Bill found his teeth, and as we returned to the lane the lorries and ambulances were moving off. We hurriedly found our vehicle and mounted, and as we looked back, the false dawn revealed a long column of the enemy passing the lane entrance. Fortunately no one seemed to notice us moving off across the fields to a road that would take us in a north-west direction, which would take us through the town of Aberville. This was fatal as we realised later; we should have made a bypass to the west, because the whole place was teeming with refugees — horses and carts, prams, bicycles and the odd car all loaded to the top with household goods; and surrounded by hundreds of human beings, young and old alike, moving out into the highways away from the advancing battle. It was terrible endeavouring to drive through the crowded roads and we could only move at walking pace. We had travelled about a mile along this long straight road lined with trees and a ditch either side. At one point, above the noise of the moving crowd, there came the sound of planes; looking up the road towards the town we could see the crowds teeming in the road and dashing for the ditches. Then the planes came into view; they came low straight up the road belching out fire and with a screaming roar they were coming at us. In a jumping rush we made for the ditches. I remember bumping into an elderly woman dressed in black and holding a shawl over her head. She fell beside a large poplar tree. I remember helping the woman to crouch closer to the tree, as a shield, and I stood over her hoping against hope that we would be safe — with the crashing of guns and the roar of the engines, the planes were past — we had seen the first of the German fighter planes, and didn't like what we saw, or what they left behind.

I gradually helped the old lady to her feet, and then she looked up into my face and I saw a face just like my own grandmother's face. I was shaken for a moment, but then she saw above her the face of a young English lad of eighteen, inexperienced in the matter of war, and possibly one that reminded her of her own son, or grandson. She clung to me crying 'merci beaucoup' and then made her way on to the road to see the carnage scattered along the road, which must have stretched at least a mile without a turn; one could see that here had been a sitting target for those young Nazi pilots. In front of our vehicle, which luckily had only suffered a few stray bullets, was a horse and cart with the horse laying dead in its shafts and the load of furniture scattered. What a sight, this seemingly endless procession of human beings; goats, cattle, with dogs barking; scores of ragged children, some pushing perambulators, bicycles, hand carts leading goats on string; tearful infants in mothers' arms; the only men seemed to be very old; and then there were the men of the church, who seemed to be sharing the same fate as the crowd, trying to give some help and support to the womenfolk.

It seemed ages before we would get clear, and when we did it was to turn into a road leading to Dunkirk. The talk among the men was that the 1st Division could make a stand some miles outside Dunkirk to allow regrouping — but little did we know that this was not the case — our main army was assembling in Dunkirk and on the beaches for evacuation.

We waited a little to the west, and for three days we remained in a wood, well away from the main road. Meanwhile one could see streams of forces making for the town. Then some artillery chaps dug in at the side of the road and two Bren gun carriers waited near the crossroads about half a mile away. Of course we heard later that they were there to make contact with the enemy when they approached, then fight a rearguard action. We heard later that the evacuation had been taking place, hence all the noise and activity over the town, which was to the east.

On the evening of June 5th, we were told that we were to work our way west taking a route away from the area known as the Somme, a name which brought back many of the stories my father had told us years before. We kept well ahead of the forces who were fighting a rearguard. We lost one medical section near Dunkirk and a missing dispatch rider turned up having thumbed a lift with a gun crew. We travelled mainly at night, and soon came within a few kilometers of Cherbourg. We moved into an orchard in the late evening. Most of the time German planes were overhead. Cherbourg lay under a blanket of smoke.

Our orders were to remain under cover away from the road, and at first light we were to put all the vehicles out of commission with sledge hammers keeping back one ambulance and two trucks, which would make a dash to the quay in Cherbourg where a trawler would wait for us, and take us aboard as soon as we could get there — this we did, and successfully reached the quay and the old trawler. We were some miles out in the channel when once again Cherbourg received a heavy raid; apparently we were not seen, and arrived safely in Southampton dirty and weary but safe.

The greeting from the local people was most warm, they took us to a nearby school, where we had hot soup, cups of tea and a blanket to help us through the night — I remember going to a nearby telephone box and telephoning my parents who had had no news of me for some weeks.

It was a wonderful feeling to know we were safely back in England —

a most selfish thought perhaps, but we were not to know the price that had been paid at Dunkirk both in men and equipment. It was some days later we realized by reading the papers the true significance of all that had happened, yet with the saving of so many men from the beaches a miracle had taken place.

We realised that we must have been almost the last to leave Cherbourg, although we later heard how the Royal Engineers remained long enough to blow up the installations before leaving for Brest, where the final evacuation would take place. We moved to Salisbury Plain the following morning, and were allowed seven days' disembarkation leave. The joy of being at home, and with a little more time to explore the huge garden with all the fruit trees well endowed with luscious fruit, everything was quite peaceful.

The daily papers brought further news of the rampaging armies of the Hun in Poland and surrounding countries. We wondered how long it would be before the enemy increased his bombing. Our fears were soon proven, and by the winter of 1940 the whole might of the German *Luftwaffe* was thrown against London and other cities and towns in the south.

Our field ambulance moved into Surrey with the armoured division to form a line of defence between the south coast and London in case the enemy should gain a foothold on our shores. From our position at the foot of Leith Hill, we could see the fires in London. Our ambulances were on full alert, so we were on stand-by, day and night. I was fortunate to have Friday, Saturday and Sunday evenings free — and made full use of my time in exploring the villages around me.

We had a fellowship in Dorking Saturday evenings and I was privileged to meet some wonderful Christian people. I was to become most conscious of the difference between chapel-going and being a Christian — I also became aware of the need for this inner peace and joy — which could only come by taking Christ at his word and allow him to live in me. I was baptised on Sunday 20th April 1941 as my witness to those present that I had accepted Christ and that I was prepared to leave everything to Him no matter what the future held. I have much to thank my Christian friends for, especially a young lady who by her living witness had shown me the way into a path of inner peace. I called her GEM for short, but it was Grace; and she with my other friends gave me more true friendship than I had ever known.

We had some lovely walks over the Surrey downs. From the top of Box Hill and Ranmor Common there was a most marvellous view of the countryside, but despite the beauty around us, our minds were often distracted by the sound of the air raid warning in the town of Dorking. Then gradually the reason for this would materialise, when far above our heads we would see squadrons of enemy bombers approaching with their fighter escort weaving about and around them. We would seek temporary cover until they had passed by on their way to London, so we assumed. Sometimes our fighter planes would rise up to meet them; then there would be a swirl of vapour trails against the blueness of the sky, and very often one would see one of the slower bombers come down in a twisting dive to crash in some distant field; others would follow, and from our shelter behind a wall, a prayer would be offered for those young men who died. Sometimes we would count the parachutes that opened out and drifted down some way away.

Saturday evenings we would enjoy our fellowship with all our friends. Then I would catch a Green Line bus, which would drop me near my headquarters in a large house in Abinger Common. One evening an enemy plane dropped a load of fire-bombs in the fields and on the road straddling the bus, which continued travelling slowly without lights until we were in the shelter of the wood-lined lane away from the main road.

Friday evenings we had an hour of fellowship in a little cottage on a farm. It was known as the 'laundry cottage', due to the fact that my friends took in washing to subsidise their meagre earnings. The Moore family were a most kind and generous family of real Christians; the warmth of their friendship has lasted almost fifty years. Alfred the youngest and only brother, suffered terribly with asthma; but despite this he would continue to play the little harmonium for our hymn singing, which would often get louder to drown the sound of enemy planes overhead. Sometimes we would hear bombs falling, counting them, as they got nearer we would blow the lamp out quickly and wait in the darkness until the next bomb had passed over us to burst with a crash in the woods beyond the farm. It was customary on Fridays to collect a basket of eggs to deliver to my friends in Dorking. I have known the time when I have had to drop into a ditch when fire-bombs rained down. More than once I had to apologise for delivering cracked eggs.

My friend Alfred was called to the Army. Due to his health he was invalided out, but not before he had met a nice young ATS girl who later became a worthy addition to the family at the 'laundry cottage'.

The people of Abinger and Dorking were to become true and constant friends over very many years. Their homes were always open to us of the medical corps.

It was a sad day when we were told that we would be moving back to Wiltshire to prepare for going overseas. Nevertheless I was privileged to spend a wonderful Christmas in Parkway, Dorking at the homes of Frank and Lillian Lewis and Lily and Les Denham — there was also Grace, and Ken my pal, who was to travel with me overseas. He remained a constant pal, and letters from Grace gave me great upliftment when I really needed it.

We eventually settled down to the usual duties in camp. We medics spent the morning training in the art of retrieving bodies from the tank through the turret by using a steel tripod and ropes; but time was to prove that this contraption was out of place when one is under shell fire, and time was somewhat at a premium. As time went on, we all learned to do things to fit the occasion — they called this initiative.

The day came when we moved to Bradford-on-Avon in Wiltshire. We made some friends here too, and once again after a few weeks found ourselves packing for overseas yet again. There were many sad goodbyes when I left the family after a 48-hour embarkation leave — Ken and his wife had gone home with me so I felt a little better as once again we walked down Clack Hill to catch the train at Dauntsey station. Promising my father and mother not to look back, we departed wondering where we would be going and if and when we would be back.

It was the following Sunday evening we marched to the train; my sister Pat, Ken's wife and Grace had spent time with us, and as we marched past them on the path near the station I remember calling out "Tat-ta see you soon". We little realised it would be some years before we would see them again.

It is inevitable that at such departures one is given small gifts to carry with one. Fred Usher, a glove maker from Bradford-on-Avon, gave me a large piece of chamois leather for various uses, including the arrest of bleeding, which he had found from personal experience. He and his wife were wonderful friends to my family, and were to give them great support during my absence and for many years afterwards. I think I should now say that I broke my watch a few days prior to leaving and my brother Douglas kindly loaned me his Ingersol pocket watch to carry with me. Through his kindness, I was able to use it to good effect when taking pulses, and when more expensive watches failed, the little Ingersol from Woolworths in Cheltenham, in a little chamois leather bag my friend made for me, continued going for over four years through some awful conditions to be eventually returned safely to its owner — but needing a good cleaning. So it was that we boarded the train for our journey to Avonmouth.

CHAPTER 12

Adventures Ahead

We sailed from Avonmouth and I remember passing down the Severn with the lights on the Welsh coast sliding past, and in the morning we passed on in sight of the Welsh coast and Snowdon in the distance — I was aware that I had never seen Wales before and hoped that one day I might be able to visit Ken and his family in the Rhondda Valley and to see those magnificent mountains in all their majesty. Another convoy of merchant ships joined us from Liverpool and with them came our escort of a cruiser, several destroyers and corvettes, and for several days we were pleased to see a Sunderland flying boat keeping a watchful eye on us. Ken and I had our own cabin with two bunks — we were most fortunate. Unfortunately the Service Corps men and those of the Tank Regiment mostly, had hammocks down in the holds amongst tanks, lorries and battle equipment. It was a marvellous experience for me, the adventure of being on a ship of this size. The SS *Orion* was a large vessel and built originally I believe as a passenger liner for the Orient Line.

Our days were spent in physical training; evenings were spent reading and writing letters which would be posted at our first port of call. We enjoyed watching schools of porpoise keeping up with us and flying fish which seemed to shoot out of the water and disappear beyond the bow. Sunrises and sunsets were magnificent; the seas were anything from gale force waves to huge swells, which seemed to swallow up the ships in the distance, and one could hear the throb of the engines and the propeller as our ship rose up onto the huge crest of a swell, and revealing a ship of the same size in the large basin of grey water. A few moments later we would be down there ourselves completely out of sight, but always in touch with the other vessels.

There were several false alarms over the weeks — U-boats had been reported off the African coast — so it was as well we had kept well off the usual shipping lanes, and were some hundreds of miles out in the Atlantic.

It was about 10.15 p.m. one night, as Ken and I were about to put our light out in our cabin, when a shudder went through the ship and the alarms went off. We immediately donned our life-jackets and made for our boat stations. We arrived to see that one of our escort vessels, the *Revenge* a cruiser of some size, was just moving away from our bows. In the manoeuvring, the *Orion* had collided with her, and had pushed her bows across the fore deck which caused quite a rupture to bow and superstructure of our ship.

Once the two vessels had parted, assessment of the damage was carried out; it was found that we were taking in water; damage having been caused down below the water-line. Everything was done to lighten the bows. So much cargo etc., was moved to the stern, including the troops — and at a decrease in knots we sailed for the nearest port in Africa — this proved to be Freetown and Sierra Leone. Here we lay-to while temporary repairs were carried out under the watchful eye of the light cruiser *Repulse*.

After a few days, we departed late in the evening, having unloaded a large consignment of mail and enjoyed the warmth of this African sun, on decks that were no longer heaving in the mighty swells of the Atlantic. We enjoyed watching the local boys diving into the water after coins thrown in by the troops, coins often referred to as Glasgow Tanners or buckshees. Here too, one was somewhat intrigued with the atmosphere and scenery; the golden beach sloping up to the density of the jungle of coconut trees and date palms. Beyond one could see forest-covered hills, and nearer to us on the left, one could see various buildings and moorings for vessels smaller than our ship.

Having left Freetown we had the pleasant experience of going 'over the line' a few days out. This was the Equator, and to mark the occasion, the well-known ceremony with Father Neptune was enacted, and quite a few of us were dropped into the swimming-pool.

We had a number of vocalists on board who were able to render suitable songs to conclude the afternoon entertainment. My pal Ken, who normally sang as first tenor, often sang a solo — his favourite piece was called *O' Lord my God when I in awsome wonder*. The words of this beautiful piece of music could be heard floating back over the decks, wafted with a gentle breeze, to men who with heads bowed seemed to be held with the beauty of the words "How Great Thou art".

So we progressed in a southerly direction once again within sight of our convoy and escorting vessels, and seldom without schools of porpoise and flying fish.

Then one morning we heard we were approaching South Africa. Ken and I made for the bows and in the early morning mist we made out the faint shape of land. We were actually coming into the Cape of Good Hope. As we approached what we eventually knew to be the entrance into Table Bay Cape Town, everyone was so filled with a longing to see Table Mountain that the ship listed to portside, so we were all asked by the captain to move to the starboard to allow the vessel to right itself; and thousands of men moved like ants to watch from all advantage points, as out of the mist we were able to see the flat top of Table Mountain gradually take shape; and as we came into the bay the sun came through the mist and then we had a view of Cape Town. As if a signal was given, all the windows began flashing in reflected sunshine. Apparently this was the custom of these wonderful people — greeting us from the Motherland.

We were hosted and toasted by many including Toc H who did us proud. HMS *Andes* was moored along side us and my pal and I had the pleasure of spending pleasant times with the first officer, who was a Toc H member.

On landing, we were amazed at the huge mounds of green oranges along the quay. My face must have shown such awe at such quantities of fresh fruit, that a kindly lady asked if I would like to try one? Naturally I could not deny this wonderful offer. I was not allowed to take an orange and peel it, as the lady promptly produced a knife and glass, and within moments I was drinking wonderful fresh orange juice. Eventually Ken, I and two other medics, were invited to the lady's home. We found that each member of a ladies' club escorted and entertained troops while they were in Cape Town. Naturally we would still be expected to sleep on board, and reported in at 11.59 p.m.

Our first day was spent at the young ladies' school at Wynneburg just outside Cape Town. Here the principal and her husband showed us around and gave us a wonderful evening meal of fresh fish and chips, a lot of fruit drinks and home-made cakes. We made friends with so many English-born folk, who remained firm friends for many years. Many, many times I was so pleased to receive bundles of the South African paper known as the *"Out Span"* from the headmistress of the school in the years to follow.

Our visit to Cape Town came to a close, and once again in the early hours of the morning the *Orion* moved from the quay and headed out to sea, to the flashing of sun on the windows in the town, and right up the mountainside and in the distance, we could hear the voice of a lady singing over a loudspeaker the nostalgic tune of *Land of Hope and Glory* — as was her custom to say farewell and Godspeed to the troops who were moving once again into the unknown future.

By late evening we were once again well out into the Atlantic. There were no lights except from the stars which seemed to move from left to right as our ship gently rolled and heaved from one huge trough to another. The only sound was the wind in the superstructure, and the throb of the distant engine as the propellers came nearer the surface at the stern.

Days passed and we moved up through the Indian Ocean. We only saw one ship going in the opposite direction. She was too far away for our eyes to identify her, but we were told that it was the *Queen Mary*. She nearly always travelled alone, her speed was a match for any U-boats that watched the shipping lanes.

Once again we enjoyed the 'crossing the line' ceremony as we travelled north over the Equator, and called into Aden, dropping off more mail, and doing a little bartering over the side of the ship. Of course now, as we moved on again, we believed with some certainty that our destination was Egypt. This belief was verified when we came in to the port of Tewfik at the southern end of the Suez Canal.

We disembarked eventually, and moved into marquee accommodation for the night. We had heard from men who had served in the Canal Zone before and had been warned to keep an eye out for thieves who would go to great lengths to steal anything from you — Army pay books, even the shirt one was wearing. So great care had to be taken.

So it was that one of our members wishing to go to the lavatories in the early hours decided to put his army cape on against the heavy rain that had been falling for some time. On his return, he fumbled his way in the dark to his sleeping spot and while crouching down to slip his boots off, the man next to him saw his crouching form and promptly brought a boot down sharply on the other chap's head thinking that we had a 'wog' in our midst — naturally the air was blue for a while.

All newcomers to Egypt were also warned to be very careful when using the latrine, which happened to be buckets under wooden seating. To empty the buckets each day, an Arab with a mule and cart would come up behind the latrine and draw the bucket out for emptying. We were warned not to be sitting while this operation took place because Arabs usually carried very sharp knives and may use them to some effect. Most rookies carried vivid pictures in their minds of what could happen. So there were lots of hasty risings at the sound of a bucket rattling to the delight of the sergeant who ran the whole length of the latrine rattling the bucket — just for a laugh at our expense.

The next morning we entrained for the north and travelled by rail following the Suez Canal towards Alexandria where we branched on to a single track to a dead-end stop called Amariya Ikingi Maru a few miles out in the desert.

Here we erected tents to hold the whole field ambulance, and for about two weeks spent our time camouflaging the vehicles and painting divisional and company signs, which we would carry with us; and besides my usual job as ambulance attendant when with HQ, I would have to make sure that our red cross signs would be erected at the side of the main road or track where we were leaguered.

We moved out to join the forward troops of the 7th Armoured Division, and as the winter offensive had begun we passed through the wire dividing Egypt from Cyrenaica some miles south of Sollum and Fort Capuzzo, which was said to be in Italian occupation. The track we were on, some miles south of the coastal road, was called C Track near Fort Madelene, and was to become well travelled and eventually so deep with dust from the thousands of wheels and tank tracks, that the movement of these could be seen ten to fifteen miles away in the shimmering heat. Our first reminder that there was a war on was one mid-morning as I sat on the front of my lorry roof, as one of the look-outs. Two German Me 109 fighters came out of the sun behind us and strafed the column, missing my vehicle but hitting two lorries in front carrying medical supplies and men, who were seen to spill over the tail-board of the lorry with blood running down their arms and legs. The planes carried on dealing with transport up ahead, and we were left to deal with the wounded while the field ambulance carried on to support those in need nearer the front. Apparently the battle was very fluid, but with a gradual advance to the west.

In the evenings very often, we would be told of our position, and what had occurred through the day. Such as the fact that we had bypassed places still occupied by the Axis Forces such as Bardia and Capuzzo, and I could possibly give a graphic account of the battle of Sidi Rezegh as the 22nd Armoured Brigade seemed to be in the fore of most of the tank battles. My diaries bring back to memory the number of tanks that brewed up, and the individual spirals of smoke that rose into the sky long after the battle had moved forward.

I will leave the historians to write their accounts of the 8th Army and its exploits. I remember almost cursing the sand that rose up around you on every movement, and the incessant flies which clung to your eyes and around your mouth for what moisture there was. You could feel them entering your mouth and they were often found in your tea. Of course flies were more plentiful where the Axis Armies had camped, especially the Italians who had a nasty habit of leaving their calling cards near a little bit of camel scrub without covering it up. As the Italian lira had little monetary value, this was often used as toilet-paper and could be seen scattered around, or waving like little flags on these little heaps of excrement. This in time would be hidden below ground by the scarab beetles or eaten by flies or covered by the periodical sandstorm. Of course several times our advance literally came out of the blue, which gave the enemy little chance of doing anything other than to grab their water-bottles and weapons, then scarper in the nearest vehicle.

It did not take us too long to acclimatise ourselves to the desert and its ways — with luck we were able to have a cup of char at 6.30 a.m., sometimes lunch at midday, and a hot meal before nightfall. When we were with our headquarters section, which was the main dressing station, this was possible; but our four sections, A.B.C.D., were advance dressing stations, and were attached to one or the other of the regiments of the 22nd Armoured Brigade or 7th Armoured Division.

We knew that the axis forces were moving back along the coast road, and at one point we broke away from the main track to cut across the desert as if to make a pincer movement. Rain held us up at one point, and we had to leaguer up for the night in a large valley in the direction of Fort Musus. In the light of the moon we settled down for the night with several guards at vantage points. Some of us sat near our wireless vehicle talking over the events of the last few days.

We had covered over five hundred miles since we passed through the wire between Egypt and Cyrenaica. The historians will have written of the various battles fought on our way. The 22nd Armoured Brigade played a major part in most of the action.

Naturally it was medical sections from our field ambulances that were attached to the forward regiments of the brigade, and would only return to the main dressing station and its workshop lorry if repairs were needed, or relief after a possible over-long period up front. Of course if casualties were heavy, then we would load as many as possible onto the ambulance. I remember having four stretcher cases and six sitting ones. It was most awkward to stand on the back step over some of the tracks we had to negotiate.

Sometimes we would stop for a moment while we gave a shot of morphine or a drink of water to those inside. So that some sort of air could pass through from the front of the ambulance, the back door would be left open, but unfortunately the infernal dust would belch inside settling everywhere. Our relief ambulance would sometimes pass us on the way up. This would allow us at least one night at HQ, although I remember we had so many ambulances damaged, that we remained at HQ just long enough to redress the wounded and replenish our water; then obtaining directions, set off to the CCS, which is casualty clearing station, some ten to twenty odd miles to the rear.

The problem was returning to our unit. We returned to find that they had moved up yet again — but by careful driving we followed in the tracks watching for directional signs — we eventually found our HQ at a place called Antelat, and we were able to get a meal of burque, pronounced bergoo, a sort of stew made from boiled army biscuits and corned beef. As the sun had sunk fairly low, we enjoyed a meal without the attention of the flies. My driver was added to the guard for the night which proved to be quiet except for a few Very lights which rose into the night sky some miles away.

The morning of 24th December came, and as usual was spent in the precincts of the leaguer doing a little washing of underpants and socks, which dried very quickly in the dry air of the desert.

In the evening, Ken and I sat just outside the wireless truck and listened to Vera Lynn singing songs that were to become so well known. It was so strange, and very sad to be so far away from our loved ones at such a time as this. I wondered what the family would be doing. My thoughts were interrupted when the padre came over to see if we would join him for carols in the morning. Of course, Ken and I always supported him when it was possible — and agreed to get the men to join us at 9 o'clock around the Red Cross area. After a while, I said goodnight to Ken and walked over to the lorry which carried our kitbags and spare equipment. Here I located my bag, and from the bottom of the bag I drew out a wooden box of sweets I had purchased before leaving England — I found them in good condition and with the aid of toilet-paper proceeded to wrap up little parcels of sweets. To these little gifts for the seven lads in my section I added packets of ten Victory V cigarettes, and then walking back through the sand to the sleeping forms of the lads, I deposited a little Christmas gift under each tin helmet.

Thanks to the bright moon I was able to carry out my mission without rousing anyone. The only person about was the guard and he stood over in the shadow of the wireless van, and was out of sight from where I was. I was in my blanket by the time he did his rounds.

A beautiful morning came — everything was so peaceful. We had a mug of tea at 6.30 a.m. and at 7 o'clock we had breakfast of tinned bacon and army Arnott's biscuits. At 9 o'clock the padre and I found a wooden box to use as an altar, and placed it near the big red cross on the ground in the centre of the leaguer. This denoted that we were covered by the Geneva Convention and we always hoped that the enemy would recognise this.

So it was that our medics and the drivers of the service corps, joined us and the carol *Hark the Herald Angels Sing* was sung followed by a short prayer by the padre. Then he invited us to gather round the altar which was the old wooden box, to partake of the Holy Sacrament — everyone came close and knelt down, the first time for some — then as we bared our heads, the padre revealed an army mug of water and some broken army biscuits. No words I write will ever express the humility, the depth of the feeling of oneness, as we accepted the bread and wine in the Saviour's name. After the 'Our Father' and the blessing, each man shook hands with the padre and with each other. Each man was alone with his own thoughts, for indeed we had just witnessed a presence which we knew would remain with us despite all our shortcomings. In the shaking of hands, with a trace of a tear in one's eyes, we lads were drawn even closer and this would help as a support to each other in the days ahead.

Shortly after Christmas we moved again and found that we were meeting more transport than usual. Later it was found that the enemy had decided to attack again from Agheila and were making for Benghazi. We were instructed to move back to give elbow room for the armour. It was an orderly and planned withdrawal and soon we had arrived at Mekili, having travelled up the Tmimi track from the desert. We bivouacked on the coastal roadside, but around two a.m. we were ordered back down the track, as the enemy had succeeded in taking most of the coast road and were within a mile or so of the Gazala crossroads just up the road. Fortunately, we were fairly safe from air attack in the dark, and finally made the desert track travelling east.

My ambulance was dispatched to support a medical section attached to the tanks, and that evening as usual the tanks formed up in two lines, the soft skinned vehicles, including my ambulance, parked between the tanks. Other tanks moved in to close the box that would give us some security for the night. Later on enemy planes dropped flares around the leaguer and one or two bombs dropped fairly close, but at least any marauding jerries could not drive our lorries or ambulances away. The guards were also kept alert for any eventuality.

In the morning, at first light, the leaguer opened up to the appropriate distance between vehicles. As one tank moved off, it was found that during the bombing the night before, a driver had slid under a tank for protection. Unfortunately the tank sank down into the sand, squashing the poor fellow into the ground. Of course even if he had cried out I doubt if the noise would have allowed his cries to be heard. This was a sad lesson to us all. We also learned not to dig our slit trenches sideways to a track, because we had one case, where a Bren gun carrier came through the camp at night, and one track sank right down into the slit trench, killing one of the lads.

But in time, our ears and senses became attuned to the sounds of the desert night. Sometimes it was almost comical to see little heads rise up from the slit trenches to have a look round. But more often, if we leaguered after dark, there was little point in digging in as we called it, and sometimes of course the ground could be very rocky, and impossible to dig.

We were still moving back eastwards and later in the day found ourselves joining thousands of other vehicles using the same track heading for the road that would take us past Tobruk. We were moving nose to tail, and everyone must have kept their fingers crossed because we were a sitting target for enemy bombers. It was a most uncomfortable situation, riding along, slipping and sliding through dust-laden tracks, faces covered with handkerchiefs, anti-gas goggles on to keep the dust out of our eyes — longing for the chance to stop and brew up. What water I had in my bottle, was hot and blackish.

Coming up to the turn off down into Tobruk itself, we came upon a military policeman vainly trying to direct each vehicle according to its corps sign to where they should go — the poor chap looked terrible smothered in dust, red eyed and shaking like a leaf on a tree — I asked my driver to pull in to one side while I went back to speak to the 'red cap', firstly to ask if he had seen anything of our field ambulance, as I was due for refueling petrol and rations. The poor chap lowered the cloth from his face and said he thought the brigade was on the desert track some miles inland. Anyway he said that he had heard that a tank battle was taking place near Knights Bridge which was south. He asked for a drink of water saying he had been on duty since first light. Twice the area had been blasted by Stukas, and as he spoke a German Junkers 88 came over on reconnaissance and went off over Tobruk; but within less than five minutes the plane had turned and came in lower. Once again this was it — we threw ourselves down amongst the rocks and sand. After the blasts we rose to see the face of the 'red cap' — his face must have reflected ours, smothered in dust with two smarting eyes. Between gasps he said "It's no good I've had enough." I then saw him kneel down again weeping — he must have been through hell itself. I estimated that he had been on these cross tracks for nearly nine hours with no water or food except those little paving slabs which took so long to masticate, in a mouth so dry, and with a tongue that must have felt like leather. I decided this chap could not be left here, and put him on the front seat with the driver while I sat in the doorway. It's as well I did, as the poor chap made an attempt to dismount and run at the least sound of gun-fire. That evening he was ferried back to a field hospital, and the following year I saw the same man doing his stuff on the main track, near Bir-Hachiem, just prior to one of the worst tank battles.

Having located our own HQ ambulance, we fueled up and collected our seven days' rations. The following morning, as we were within about two miles of the Mediterranean, we took our ambulance off the road to walk down to the water. We simply walked straight in, having dropped our clothes nearby — we then dried in the sun, and then Will, my driver and I, carried two of my stretchers down to the water, and with handfuls of wet sand, we did our best to clean off the blood that had accumulated there. It was well and truly dried in, but after a good soaking, they at least smelt better.

Back in HQ we received orders almost immediately to report to the 3rd C.L.Y.s in the forward position. On arriving they were still in action. We found their support groups in a wadi where four tanks in reserve were waiting just below the escapement — a tank commander was stood on the turret of one tank watching the battle, and taking stock of the situation. About half a mile away, a tank was burning; one tank had its track damaged and had been put out of commission. We saw the look-out jump down and come running over to say that the men on the knocked out tank were wounded and were sheltering behind the tank and would we collect them. A tank commander said he would drive forward if we could drive closely to him. So using his tank as a shield, we were able to get within yards of the wounded men. Two stretcher cases were hastily loaded. The walking wounded grabbed their arms, and within half an hour we had returned to the wadi, thanks to the tank who shielded us to and from the scene of battle.

The moans of ricochetting shells seemed to be coming closer and we noticed several 25-pounder guns moving over to our left. Within a short time they had got their guns into position and had started firing over our heads, onto the enemy.

With my ambulance full, I started out for our main dressing station. By late afternoon, I had transferred my wounded. I returned to the medical section still attached to the depleted, yet surviving tanks of the C.L.Y.

While we were in the process of brewing up, as we had missed a meal while travelling, my ambulance was needed to help the driver of a fifteen-hundredweight truck who had driven onto a mine — his legs had caught the full blast and both legs were off just below the knee. With care we dressed his wounds and after injecting morphia, brought him back to our first aid post, which was only a truck with a sheet hung down one side to shield us from the sun. In this shelter, we were able to attend to his badly mauled legs. By cutting away his clothing, we were able to tidy up the torn flesh and pad him up well with vaseline, gauze and sulphonamide powder. This we had learned to do with so many wounded — cover the dressings with plaster of Paris dressing, which we found was the only way to keep the flies off, and lessen the chance of gangrene. The patient had been conscious most of the time, and was able to answer a few questions. I lit a cigarette, and put it to his lips, and then gave him a sip of tea — shortly after which he went to sleep. We gave him a transfusion and the doc asked me to remain with him while he went to find out our present situation. He returned at dark to say that the main dressing station was moving back and that we should report back as soon as our duties allowed. At dark the tanks had withdrawn and were moving back past us in the moonlight. It was very quiet through the night, and as I watched over the patient, after changing the drip I sat and listened to his mutterings of "Diane, Diane". It must have been his wife's name. We dare not move him in his present condition. I hoped he would come out of his stupor before daybreak; but in the false dawn, he became quiet and his pulse became weak. Doc came in, and after an examination said that the man would not recover. My driver brewed up and we were drinking this when the sound of vehicles came from a mile or so up front — it was the engines of heavy stuff, and seemed to be moving along the skyline. Our patient passed away, and the three of us did what was necessary with his personal belongings and then buried him in the lee of a small hill, away from the track, having marked the spot with some rocks and a spot on my map. We then got ready to retreat with the regiment. Doc, as usual, would be left with the problem of writing to his next of kin.

We seemed to travel over endless waste, and at noon passed through a leaguer of tanks and artillery. The tanks belonged to the Gloucester Hussars. We had barely cleared the leaguer when we noticed men running, I pulled up and realised a mass of Stukas were heading our way. Of course all this build up of vehicles was too good a target to miss, and they took advantage of it.

We left our seats and dived under the ambulance as the first bombs landed — what with the whine of engines, the rattle of guns, the answering chatter of Bren guns, it was best to put our fingers in our ears. Then through the silence that followed came the cries and calls for help. I felt the side of my head wet, and after a moment realised I had not been hit, but shrapnel had pierced the side of my ambulance smashing a stretcher in two, and had broken a large bottle of acriflavine which I kept for dressings. We were needed elsewhere — utter carnage — thank God the Hun did not return until evening —

we were able to lay out the dead. Among them was one of their senior officers from my own county of Gloucestershire.

Passing this spot the following year I found that the engineers had constructed a large cross out of petrol cans which everyone would see from the main track. Although our section had lost no one, my ambulance was the only one that had received damage to one side, but it was still drivable, so we loaded up the sitting wounded and left the regiment to return to our main dressing station; the 2nd Light Field Ambulance, who were still moving in retreat when eventually we caught up with them. We had two broken springs on the rear, but were not allowed to halt for repairs. We were ordered to make for a casualty clearing station fourteen miles south-east — we gradually left the sights and sounds of vehicles and found ourselves quite at peace as we scanned the horizon for our destination, which we eventually did. After we had handed over the wounded, and had a hot meal, we started back to find HQ somewhere to the east.

My pal arrived back about the same time absolutely exhausted. At Bir El Gobi he stopped to go to the assistance of another ambulance that had driven twenty yards onto a minefield. Typical of Ken, he had walked in the tracks of the stranded ambulance, climbed in the back door to discuss the situation with the driver to plan a way to save both the patients and the men in the ambulance. Keeping in the wheel tracks, Ken then backed his ambulance up until the ambulances were close together. The stretcher cases were then transferred and eventually both ambulances were safely back in the main track. I heard afterwards that he had actually guided the last ambulance by standing on the back step to give directions. He showed remarkable courage on another occasion such as this, and carried a wounded man on his shoulders away from a minefield — when asking him how it could happen, he modestly said, "Ah well queer things can happen in a sandstorm." And I was to learn this myself later on.

At a place called Knights Bridge, during a sandstorm, my friends reported a German soldier directing one of our convoys — this was not impossible because they had as many of our vehicles which they had captured as we had of theirs. It was often a case of hit or miss and sometimes identification came too late. But in a sandstorm there is always the chance to get going, making sure of course that you go in the right direction. In quite a thick sandstorm one evening we drew in, and leaguered up beside the main track. On the other side of the track there was our equipment some thirty feet high, about fifty yards away. There was a jumble of boulders at the foot of the escapement, and as we had arrived here during a lull we decided to brew up, and move on in the morning.

It was while I waited in the queue for breakfast that I looked towards the rock pile, when a movement caught my eyes. I saw someone peeping over the boulders at us. So pretending to read a piece of paper I made sure I wasn't imagining things and counted three German soldiers with their picket infantry caps on. I collected my mug of tea and then ambled on to our dental officer who was sitting out of sight of the Germans — I explained what I had seen and we both spied on the situation from under a vehicle. I am sure the poor chaps had become separated from their regiment in the sandstorm the previous evening — and I could imagine how much they wished they could share our tea and biscuits. Anyway it was not long before they were rounded up and put in the bog — I expect they were pleased to feel that their war was over.

There were lots of personal experiences, insignificant to some, but to me they would remain as little stepping-stones through six and a half years of war.

On one occasion I remember scrambling out of my ambulance on to a pile of rocks, when some Me 109s came in strafing, only to find that a rock I had my hand on moved and looking up I found my hand had been resting on a large tortoise. This was near El-Aden air strip — I could only presume that it had been a pet of some Italian while in occupation. I couldn't help wondering what the poor thing lived on in this arid waste of sand, and rock, and I carried nothing with me other than corned beef and army biscuits. The one biscuit I tossed to him as I remounted my ambulance would last him for days.

A few days later I found a chameleon in a bush of camel scrub. I managed to tie a small piece of string round its neck and allowed it a ride in the driving compartment. He did his disappearing act several times, but by following the string I could find him. Food was plentiful and he had quite a capacity for the millions of flies that hung around previous campsites.

Another little episode was while we were near Fort Mesus. The fort lay south of Benghazi, some way out in the desert near one of the main east to west tracks. It was off this track that we leaguered the second day of retreat and in the evening we lads sat near the wireless truck waiting for any item of news that may come through. Around midnight, my friend and I went to find our blankets. On the the way over we became aware of a movement of traffic using the track we were near, and coming from the west, where lay the enemy. Our curiosity got the better of my pal Charlie, so he and I ambled to within fifty yards and stood to watch the column go past — but go past they did not — they stopped, and troops began to dismount, and then we heard men calling to one another in German. At the sound of those guttural voices, Charlie and I dropped on our faces behind some camel scrub, and lay there watching the Hun relieving themselves. After a while, laughing and calling to one another, they once again loaded up — then with sidelights on they continued past us. This was quite a large column of armoured cars and lorries, followed by artillery and limbers. When the last vehicle had passed, we rose and went to report to the officer of the guard. The colonel told the officer we would start at first light, and endeavour to keep out of the way of the German flying column until we were able to obtain information as to the situation. Everything was so fluid, everyone was on lookout; there was much movement away to the north-west according to the dust clouds, and to our right, some ten to fifteen miles away, one could see the light tops of trucks moving east in line with us; they later dropped out of sight behind a ridge.

By mid-morning we came to a large wadi into which we descended, and after two or three hundred yards ascended up onto the plateau. Having all negotiated the steep side of the wadi, we moved ahead slowly, while the OC got his bearing.

It was only by chance that one of those in the rear truck glanced back across the waste to see that a German force had arrived up through the valley. An armoured car with pennant flying was about to make an attack, and its first traces went past my ambulance to land near the colonel's truck. Needless to say everyone got moving — the ground conditions prevented any speed over thirty miles an hour — but luck was on our side, for some reason the armoured car seemed to wait for the remainder of his column — I gathered his warning shots were meant to halt us, as to capture a complete field ambulance would have been a great help to him, with our present supply of petrol and water.

But this day was ours, and in mid-afternoon a Kitty Hawk did a short landing, supplying us with information and new map references — we were on radio silence apparently due to the distance from our main force, but by travelling late into the night, we were able to cover much ground and eventually arrived in our rightful position about ten miles to the rear of the armour and forward forces — on the other hand our ambulances were attached to the forward units. In February our colonel notified us that he had been promoted to A.D.M. services and would be leaving shortly. He would be terribly missed. He was one of the gentlemen who was a friend to everyone — a wonderful surgeon. More than once I found myself laying close to him when diving for the only vacant slit trench.

Our corps commander was Lieutenant-General Willoughby Norris, 30th Corps. He could not have been a better commander. He was to become a good friend of mine. Strange to say both he and Lady Norris were to become patients of mine some years after the war. I also had the privilege to remain friends with doctors and my pals who had served in the R.A.M.C through the war — but sad to say more than half of our lads were no longer with us. My pal Basil, was captured with his section, and eventually moved from the desert to Italy. I traced him through the Red Cross and wrote letters to him when possible.

We were most fortunate in having several Christian pals — their inner strength was a source of help to many especially the wounded. On one occasion our padre was blown up by a mine and the colonel gave Ken permission to take his place until a replacement came — of course it was not always possible to have a priest on hand when burying the dead — we all did this act as a part of our duty to the dead; and as Christians, we did this with dignity and love. I remember, I was challenged by an N.C.O. for using a clean blanket to wrap a body in for burial. We were supposed to use only blankets that were soiled, or ones we had acquired from the enemy; but I must confess the situation was such that I gave no thought to this order — in haste, I did what was necessary, then mounted up and tried to catch up with my unit.

Still in retreat, we moved along the coastal road towards Egypt, and eventually passed places that would become etched in the memories of thousands of troops in their journeys up and down the desert. Tobruk, Sidi Rezegh, Acroma, Bardia, Fort Capuzzo, Hell Fire Pass and over the escarpment to Sollum in the valley near the sea. Halfaya Pass or Hell Fire Pass, as we knew it, was a steep hill comprising of several hairpin bends and had to be treated with great respect. An ack-ack regiment was on the brow of the hill. Ghurkhas were dug in also, and were able to give air defence for those using the pass.

Passing through Sollum, we passed Sidi Barrani, then Mersa Matruh, and in the following days we arrived at El Alamein, where apparently our army were going to help reform, and prepare a line of defence. This was undertaken by 30th Corps under General Willoughby Norris, who did a fine job of improving our defence, intending to do the enemy as much damage as possible. If he made any attempt to force his way to the Canal Zone, one prisoner of war had said (as only a German could) that Rommel would crush the 8th Army and take the Canal Zone, and later the Suez would be theirs.

Our brigade had suffered heavy losses in men and material; those who had survived joined forces with the 4th Brigade and settled in south of El Alamein. Our field ambulance was relieved and sent back to Alexandra to re-equip, and we moved into a camp at Sidi Bish outside Alex. Here we settled in and enjoyed the luxury of hot showers, regular meals and peaceful nights.

Our new padre, Ken and I, made frequent visits to Alexandra to share Christian fellowship with men of all classes and from different regiments, including the Navy and Air Force. I met an old pal in a cafe in Alexandra. He came from Northleach and owned the garage where I had stopped for petrol and repairs. Some years after the war I was glad to meet him and know that he had survived, as did my pal Bill with whom I had joined up. One of our luxuries was to call in at the YMCA for a meal, and soak up the carefree atmosphere shared by all the young lads after the trauma of the last months in the desert.

My pal Bill, was extremely lucky to be sitting there with us. Twice he had been captured, and twice he had managed to escape. His section, when attached to the tanks, was overrun by the 21st Panzer Division. The Germans had left the Italians to guard the British, and during the early hours of the morning Bill, and his mates, hid in an Italian lorry, and when the area became busy with movement they simply drove slowly away, and eventually reached our lines. The second time Bill and his medical section drove into a German infantry brigade equipped with trucks with British divisional signs on. They realised their mistake too late. The same night Bill used the darkness to crawl into a slit trench, hoping he could hide there when the Germans moved on. But a German felt the call of nature, and walked over and started watering the camel scrub bushes with which Bill had covered himself. This was too much for Bill, and coughing and spluttering he gave himself away; even the German guard laughed. Guard duties were again handed over to the Italians to allow the Germans to pursue the British.

On this occasion it was a sandstorm that gave, not just Bill, but the whole medical section, the chance to escape. They actually used their own 15-cwt truck and a Bedford QL lorry to make their move. The German column started up and prepared to move off, leaving the Italians to guard the prisoners. But the column started off and our lads simply fell in behind. After observing the direction the column was taking our lads allowed it to draw ahead, then the 15-cwt leading, headed off to the south away from the main tracks — they made for what they hoped would be our front line. They saw several lots of vehicles leaguered away in the distance. Even with glasses, identification was difficult. Another few miles east and then a dust cloud was seen away in the distance; the attention was on this, when from a wadi to the right came two armoured cars. They came forward and stopped about a hundred yards away, and waited for our lads to identify themselves. This was done by Bill dismounting and walking forward waving his arms. Minutes later there was much relief as they were welcomed back into our lines. It was a New Zealand regiment that was holding this position, and it was with them our lads stayed the night and enjoyed their first good meal for days.

It was here my driver and I caught them up. We had seen the palm tree and swastika sign on a lorry in a convoy, so we too made off in a southerly, then gradually easterly, direction, and were fortunate to arrive at the New Zealanders' leaguer.

Once again we were able to swap experiences and supply information on the enemy movements. I think the RAF were glad to know where the enemy were. It was uplifting to see squadrons of Marrilands and Bostons go over, and see the attacks on the enemy.

Our stories were almost unbelievable, and often tinged with sadness when we thought of the lads we had lain side by side in graves a little way off the track, marked with a heap of rocks or a cross — if there was time to make one. The important thing was to leave some identification, normally one of the soldier's ID tags, then mark the spot on your OS map. It was particularly moving when we laid to rest lads who had been with us since the beginning of the war. I remember a friend who simply appeared to be resting on his back at the side of his ambulance; his helmet lay near, and his face looked completely at peace, though covered in dust. It was only when I turned him on his side to put a blanket round him that I saw the gaping hole in his back, and the large area of blood-soaked sand where the thirsty desert had swallowed up his precious life's blood. The shrapnel had taken one of my dearest pals. His name was Bernard Kirby. I had known him and his young wife a long time. This indeed was going to be a bitter pill. Someone would have to pass on the sad news. Padre Baker had the unenviable task of writing to parents and sweethearts on occasions like that. After his departure to hospital, following his episode with a landmine, the colonel usually officiated.

I felt rather bitter to think that so many of our close friends had left us in this God-forsaken land of desolation. Such were my thoughts, yet I did not really believe that we were forsaken. I knew that we all had an inner feeling of His presence and trusted in His promises, I WILL NEVER LEAVE YOU OR FORSAKE YOU. But just for a moment all I could see was yet another young life gone; to lay here at rest with others of his age in peaceful repose, unaware of the battles and death and destruction that would pass over their lonely graves in the months to come. The passing troops would turn to gaze at the little mound of rocks with a rough wooden cross. The only mark, and a mark on our map, in this great expanse known as the Western Desert.

Such were our thoughts and memories as we guiltily sat and drank cool drinks, going over past episodes, some almost unbelievable.

After a fortnight at Sidi Bish the field ambulance moved to Beni-Usef on the Sweet Water Canal a few miles out of Cairo.

It was here we completed our refit. In the few days we were free to visit Cairo, we went to the pyramids and the Sphinx. We were able to climb up inside the large pyramid to see the tomb of one of the ancient kings; it was wonderful for me to actually stand and put my hand on the huge granite blocks that the pyramid was built of. To think that I was standing where thousands of slaves had carried out the task of building such an immense building as this — one of the seven wonders of the world — at what cost in lives? This was a part of history. Now in this year of 1942, another sacrifice was being paid in the defence of this country of Egypt and its historical past and the freedom of our peoples.

CHAPTER 13

The Beginning of the End

With new men and equipment we eventually left the Canal Zone and once clear of the area, moved across the desert, a compass bearing towards the new line at El Alamein.

I must now record just another experience we had on our way — we left the delta and as we proceeded, rose up on to a plateau and we progressed over very rocky ground where vehicles had not gone before. To prove this point we found in front of us a sea of shells like ammonites about three inches across, and about one inch thick — there were no tracks other than ours and our lorry wheels sank into the lovely white shells to a depth of about six inches — the scene to me was fantastic, a sea of whiteness; brilliant because of the sun and untouched for possibly millions of years, because indeed this must have been the sea bed, possibly at the time of the Ark. I have regretted many times that I did not halt my ambulance to collect some shells to bring home. Having arrived at our map reference we set about digging in and awaited the day when we would advance and drive the enemy right out of North Africa. General Montgomery said there was to be no stopping or going back.

October 23rd came; through the day we had watched men cleaning their weapons and collecting their bottles of water and rations; in the evening we sat around chatting — we all knew what was about to happen. At precisely 9.30 p.m. the heavens lit up, and guns stretching for miles to left and right belched forth, and although they were at least a mile in front of us, in the light of continuous gun flashes, we could see a mass of tanks waiting for the sappers to clear a gap in the minefields that lay in between us and the enemy. Parties of infantry went past, and I could not help but wonder how many of them would be left on the field in the morning. October 24th saw my section move forward about a mile.

Regimental stretcher-bearers carried seventy-three wounded back to us, now dug in between two minefields. Our ambulance carried them back to our dressing station where my friends operated and re-dressed them before sending them on to the C.C.S. Days later we were sent in to collect wounded, and found that every ambulance of the 2nd Light was needed to relay late in to the night. Three hundred and thirty-six wounded were attended to — no one had stopped for food, and I remember laying under my ambulance eating corned beef from its tin, hoping that we would get some sleep — there had been little since the battle started; of course what we really needed was a chance to take our boots off and wash our feet.

The next week we continued to do our job, for which we had been trained. At one point we were down to our last bottle of dried blood at our dressing station. Fortunately the supply lines were good, and each time I took my wounded in, someone restocked my first aid kit while I went to get a mug of tea at the kitchen wagon, and report to the sergeant-major — he was always kept informed about the condition of my section up with the tanks.

In the following weeks we moved back through the wire into Cyrenaica and on to El-Agheila in Libya, South of Benghazi nearly six hundred miles from El Alamein. It was from El-Agheila that Rommel had broken through in the spring and had driven us back to Egypt. Now at last the tide had turned for us.

The field ambulance was relieved in early December, and we moved back by coastal road in easy stages. One night we parked, and being dark, we simply wrapped up in our blankets and were soon asleep. In the morning to my surprise I found I was sleeping at the side of a grave in the village graveyard of Cirene — just off the coastal road — my thoughts turned to the crucifixion, because it was Simon of Cirene who had offered to carry the cross for Jesus.

The following day we moved on and eventually camped at another well-known place called Barce. I had been feeling sick for a few days, and as my ambulance was not being used, I decided to see my medical officer. Much to my surprise he asked me to collect my kit and report to the casualty clearing station at Tobruk. I remember how weak and nauseated I felt. On my sick report he had written Infected Hepatitis or Jaundice — I later learned that a large number of men had gone down with this complaint partially due to living on fat corned beef etc. I remember travelling by ambulance asking to stop once or twice to vomit. I felt awful, and was pleased when I was carried into the tented ward and allowed to sleep on a stretcher for the night. It was around midnight that a medical officer came round to examine me. An orderly brought me a drink then armed me out to the latrine; he then settled me for the night saying it was a rotten way to be spending Christmas Eve. I had forgotten it was actually Christmas Eve — despite feeling rotten, I remember praying for my loved ones at home, and in my mind could hear them singing carols around the piano at home.

I woke in the morning to the voice of the orderly who took my temperature, washed my hands and face, then brought me a cup of tea — he said I would be leaving by Red Cross train mid-morning.

Just before leaving we patients received a Christmas present each, which comprised of a bag made of flowered material containing a pair of socks, a bar of soap and a flannel, and a little sewing set. A card wishing me a Happy Christmas from a Mrs Foot of Devizes in Wiltshire, who belonged to the forces help society was included. I felt really touched to think these items had come from within a mile or two of my home.

An ambulance took me to the train, and met a sister of the QAIMNS who would escort us back to base hospital. It was wonderful to hear a woman's voice. Even the hard boiled eggs and plain bread were gorgeous. Thank God for bread. But what a way to leave the campaign — the war was at least six hundred miles away and here was I, sick with jaundice. It wasn't until later I learned how dangerous a complaint it is.

Occasionally my mind would have fleeting glimpses of things I had seen and witnessed, the desert held many wonders — there were the mirages, a wonderful phenomenon — something that appeared as a sea of shining water — sometimes it seemed ages before one reached the edge of this nothingless sea. Then the more grotesque shapes would gradually appear, sometimes these moving specters would turn out to be a camel train, a herd of goats, or even a vehicle on the move. On these occasions one would be filled with some trepidation until the vehicles had identified themselves.

I remember at one time we were travelling over a wide expanse of an undulating rocky plateau and sandy wadis, when suddenly one could see a single form appear from over the rim of an escapement. It would be a camel and its owner, sometimes in charge of a herd of sheep and goats. But we had no idea where they came from or where they were going, hundreds of miles from any habitation.

But the Bedouin were wonderful people, and knew the desert and its character. Several times when short of water I was directed to a little well. Of course we always carried out a test on the water as it was well known that many of the wells had been contaminated by the enemy. I once found a dead camel in one well. It was rather startling to find two large nostrils looking up through the water at you.

Reference of anything outstanding was reported and shared with other ambulances. Our drivers of the Royal Army Service Corps were great, they didn't have to be asked to help with the wounded. We all worked together wonderfully well, and shared our rations even down to the last drop of water — of course this was against the rules really — water was a person's most precious possession, but we medics carried spare for washing out wounds etc. I was rebuked once by someone for offering a German a drink. He, with hundreds had been taken prisoner, and had been told to march to the rear in the charge of three Tommies leading the way along one of the main tracks, known as C Track which was a deep rutted sea of thick dust where every movement sent clouds of dust into the air. It was hell in the heat and dust, and the incessant attention of flies was unbearable.

Anyway I felt it my duty to assist in any way I could to give some relief to the wounded of both friend and enemy alike. Now all this was pictures and memories, which would return to my mind so often over the years ahead.

CHAPTER 14

A Long Journey Home

The train eventually reached its destination and I was again carried by ambulance to No.1 General Hospital at Kantara not far from Alexandria. It was past midnight, but the orderly who greeted me and got me into bed, was such a great help to me and was to become a firm friend in the years ahead. It was wonderful to be in between white linen sheets. Having had a bed bath and hot drink, I was in the lap of luxury and lost consciousness until around 6.30 a.m. when I was woken by the day staff for a wash and a cup of tea.

After a fortnight in hospital most of my friends and I were sent to a convalescent camp. Here I caught up on all my correspondence and wrote to all the friends who had sent me air mail lettercards and parcels while in the desert. The post delivery had been such a boost to morale to men who were under a great deal of strain and deprivation.

It was in the convalescent camp that I met my friend Frank; he had played for the Saints at Southampton prior to the war, and was still very keen on football. We travelled together to the R.A.M.C. Depot at Abyssia near Cairo, and settled in to parades and lectures. But when the officer commanding found out that we had served up in the desert we were excused most duties, which I thought was very good of him.

We were all called on parade one Friday morning, and each man was asked his age and service. Frank and I were two of the youngest but had served the longest. Our names were taken and later we were asked if we would consider doing medical work aboard ships. We decided to give it a bash, as Frank put it, and on the Monday morning we were to move out by lorry to the docks at Alexandria. Meanwhile we made good use of our time visiting Cairo and the YMCA.

Having reported to the officer-in-charge on the docks at Alexandria, Major Short, Frank and I found ourselves in charge of the sick bay on a cargo vessel. We sailed on the evening tide and headed west on the Mediterranean. Three days out the look-out shouted ''MINE'' and on looking to starboard we could see a mine with its deadly prongs moving up and down in the swell about a hundred yards out. Each time it rose into view it seemed to have drawn nearer to us, and as we changed course a little we were relieved to see it moving past our stern. Several men stood by with rifles but for some reason or another did not fire. We were told afterwards that an explosion would have alerted enemy U-boats. We arrived in the Grand Harbour in Malta on 22nd February, 1943 to the sound of ack-ack guns. German planes were just departing after a raid.

It was good to get ashore, and out of the way of the troops and stevedores who were in a hurry to unload the cargo before the Hun decided to call again. A vehicle had been dispatched to collect us and take us to the Military Hospital at M'tarfa.

We moved off up through the streets of Valletta from the docks — streets that were piled high with masonry — the damage was unbelievable. We gradually made our way out into country lanes bordered with little terrace fields encircled with low stone walls, with the odd prickly pear bush or cactus leaning over. There was a Maltese woman with a herd of goats at the side of the road; a sight which was so peaceful and almost made one forget the devastation in the city and the reason why I should be there at all. Ahead could be seen the bastions of the walled city of M'dina and the town of Rabat through which we would travel to reach our destination.

Arriving at the 90th General Hospital, we were asked to report to the company office where we each gave our report and army credentials. The major asked the sergeant-major to organise a meal for us, then show us around the hospital. This was most interesting. There were surgical and medical wards in the main block; theatre and path' labs and a children's ward; also a ward for TB patients; and over in the barrack area a one hundred bedded block for fevers and convalescents.

At the completion of our inspection, we made our way back to the office where the major said ''Well lads! What do you think of the place?'' We replied that we had enjoyed our visit and thanked him for the refreshments. To our surprise he asked if we would like working in a hospital again and said the choice was ours, or did we wish to return to the Middle East and try to catch up with our unit which was poised to make the final push against Rommel in North Africa.

With the possibility of regular meals, a bath, and a bed to sleep on, this made up our minds for us. So it was arranged that we should report for duty the following morning. We soon settled in to a routine. Getting to know the staff and being able to attend to dressings and cleanse wounds without the attention of incessant flies and sand, was such relief. Our qualifications allowed us to take a responsible position, and there was the opportunity to study in greater depth both in surgery and medical. I thought I would take advantage of this, hoping that it would help me when I eventually returned to civilian life. So it was thanks to the encouragement I received that I did, with much studying and hard work, pass my finals.

In what time I had to spare, it was my pleasure to explore this lovely little island. I joined the church in the hospital grounds, Padre Mahon was our minister, and a great Christian friend he became. We had a Christian Endeavour Group, and on Sunday evenings we would travel to Floriana, just outside Velletta, to The Gospel Rooms, where there was a complete uplifting experience of rebirth. An experience I would not have missed for the world. These men came in from all three services. One young man was a deep sea diver — his time was spent salvaging cargo from vessels that were sunk in the Grand Harbour — not a pleasant task when enemy planes were overhead. He had remarkable courage. Then there was a bank manager with his wife and three children. We had the pleasure of having General Dobbie, the Governor of Malta, who was a Brother of the Plymouth Brethren, a wonderful Christian and witness to his Lord, and a wonderful inspiration to those under his command. We were to meet again after the war, and in different circumstances, at a reunion in London.

So it was a great and new experience to be working in such wonderful company, and as for the people of Malta, they were most kind, a wonderful friendly people, and I was proud to have known them as my friends. I realized that one day the war in Europe would end and I would have to leave it all behind not without a tinge of sadness, and the comradeship is something not easily replaced. Yet how I longed to see my family whom I had seen little of in six and a half years.

I made the most of my time sightseeing and taking photographs, which I would be able to share with others, I visited the little peninsula of Senglea, which seemed to have taken the brunt of the attack — it was devastated. I spent a while with a priest who told me of some of the most awful experiences; how he with his bare hands moved masonry to help children who were entombed and take them out into the safety of a cave out in the countryside; returning to work at the side of the ambulance service and defence corps day and night to bring succour and solace to the injured, the dying and bereaved. He was the typical example of the Maltese people. I thanked the Lord that He directed my path to this lovely little island where I was to spend the next two years.

I was invited to visit the Mosta Dome, the third largest dome in the world. It was a remarkable church with some of the most wonderful paintings that I had ever seen. Even this was not allowed to miss the attention of the enemy — a five hundred pound bomb pierced the dome hitting the stone floor. It skidded over the floor to finally rest against the wall where it was rendered harmless by the bomb disposal team. It still rests there as a reminder of those dark days in Malta.

In 1945, I married a sister in the QAIMNS, expecting to continue our service together and myself possibly to continue studying for advanced qualifications in medicine. But I was told that in August my army service time abroad was completed, and that we would be returning to England.

Plans were made for our departure. There were lots of farewells to make, and eventually the morning arrived when we would travel to the docks where the *Norway Princess*, a troop-ship, was laying at berth. At the last minute, my wife was requested to escort several sick female patients back by air from Luqa, so we adjusted our arrangements and planned to meet at our home near Lyneham aerodrome in Wiltshire.

As for my journey, it was quite pleasant — we sailed to the South of France and arrived at Toulon. Here we moved gently through the half submerged ships of the French navy which had been scuttled earlier in the war. After landing we were driven to a small transit camp which happened to be just outside the town. We were to stay there the night then proceed to Calais by rail. The journey was not without its excitement — we had many stops and starts for various reasons — then just after midnight the train slowed down to possibly enter a station. I rose to look out only to find the train moving gently over a trestle where the hillside had fallen away, possibly due to bombing or mines. Looking down one could see very faintly through a thick mist, a ribbon of water wandering through a valley hundreds of feet below. We were most pleased to move from this area and get on our way.

The following day we arrived in Newhaven, and then travelled to Aldershot and our depot at Crookham camp. How lovely it was to see the countryside, and the excitement was intense as we heard the familiar sound of a bugle sounding 'cookhouse'. We dismounted outside the company office, where to my surprise, I saw a Major Bernard Debenham, a friend of mine coming from his quarters. After renewing our friendship we went our separate ways and were not to meet again until November 1970, when we met at a remembrance service in the town of Wantage in Berkshire, as it was then.

Meanwhile, back at our depot we had a meal. Then one or two of the lads and I went to telephone our families and to tell them we would be arriving home later that evening. My train would be leaving for Paddington around five-thirty, so we lads went to say goodbye to all those we had travelled with from Malta. It was rather moving because we had served quite a long time together — especially my old pal Bill Hill — he had arrived at camp a few days earlier. His story was a little different to mine, because when I had left the 22nd Light Field Ambulance to go to hospital at Tobruk, he remained with them to go into the landings of Italy, then back home for the Normandy landings. And what stories he had to tell! But as we held each other's hands in farewell and with tears in our eyes (quite unashamedly), reverently we said 'thanks be to the God who gave us the attention of his undying love, and the care and keeping through some of the most trying years of our lives'.

Eventually we received our warrants and a pass for a twenty-eight day disembarkation leave, after which I was instructed to proceed to the Queen Victoria General Hospital at Netley in Hampshire. I caught my train for London and made my connection at Paddington station. My train was on time, and at 5.30 p.m. started on the final journey home. We moved through the beautiful scenery of Berkshire with its Downs bathed in the late afternoon sunshine, gently pulling into Swindon junction where there was the hustle and bustle of moving service personnel. No one seemed interested in me as I leaned out of the carriage door. Why should they? After all they too had a life to live, and a story to tell, and at last the war was over, thank God.

The train stopped briefly at Wootton Bassett, then it sped on with steam and smoke streaming along above. It began to coast along, and gradually eased gently into the little station at Dauntsey. I thought what a great thing of beauty the engine was as she stood steaming, and so lovely and dirty, smelling of oil and coal — and she had carried me home — and she was a part of my England — I suppose I was always a little sentimental.

I left my kitbag with the station master to be collected, and started to walk up the hill to my home in the village of Bradenstoke. It was a good mile of uphill climb, and as I reached the brow I stopped to look back down to the station where I could just see the roof of the train still standing at the platform, appearing not to be in any hurry to proceed on its way to the towns to the west. Trying to adjust my thoughts, I wondered if I would wake up to find everything a dream? I took in the vision of a beautiful country lane. With tears in my eyes, I realised this is what I had prayed for. My thoughts were interrupted by the voice of a gentleman bidding me "Good evening". I returned his greeting and bent down to pat the head of his dog which had come forward to greet me also. Yes, it was indeed a good evening, and I was filled with a sense of wonder and excitement as I continued my way. I became aware of more voices coming towards me, then as I drew near to the shadowy forms, I heard the words "Is that you Bern?" It was the voice of my dear mother coming out of the gloom. It was then that I knew at last I was home. One could wonder what the future held for us, but for the present, I was in a state of great joy and anticipation. My dreams had come true.

EPILOGUE

It is now fifty years since I joined the Territorial Army Volunteer Reserves, and became No. 580224 of the Military Hospital Reserves, from which I transferred to the Regular Army, and became regular No. 7519501.

I have much to thank the Royal Army Medical Corps for. Mainly in my studies in medicine, and to qualify both in medical and surgical cases, and to achieve the standards and ideals that are covered by our code of ethics. I shall ever remain grateful to the tutors and medical officers who gave so much of their time teaching us, and to the surgeons at the 90th General Hospital Malta, for allowing me the benefit of their experiences. I am still proud of the R.A.M.C. whose motto is *Inardis Fedelis*, which means "Faithful Under Difficulties" and indeed they were, and would often work far and beyond what was asked of them and under the most difficult and dangerous conditions. I shall remember the men of the 2nd Light Field Ambulance for their staunch comradeship while with the 22nd Armoured Brigade and 7th Armoured Division, for it was a time that will live on in the annals of history.

Looking back over the years I think I can say that it has been a full life. Not everything to my credit, for on one occasion in a moment of foolishness I failed a very dear friend. It was a bitter lesson to me and the regret was to remain with me always; but I learned to think, and often accept advice before acting. I hope that I had the good grace to have more care; show more compassion when it was expected of me for friend and foe alike, as we were taught; and I pray that no one was any the worse for having known me.

Talking of praying, this is something we all had in common. We would pray over our dead, we would pray for the wounded, acknowledging the Father, who despite our weaknesses and failings, brought us through the day and gave us safe lodging through the night. Believing in His forgiveness and abiding Love, I am grateful for this opportunity to share with you my thoughts and experiences, and may I leave with you the following verses;

When sinks the soul, subdued by toil to slumber,
Its closing eye looks up to Thee in prayer.
Sweet the repose beneath Thy wings o' shading,
But sweeter still to wake and find Thee there.

So shall it be at last, in that bright morning,
When the soul waketh, and life's shadows flee;
O' in that hour, fairer than daylight dawning,
Shall rise the glorious thought — I AM WITH THEE.

SYNOPSIS OF SERVICE

Born	Northleach, Glos. — 11 . 12 . 1919.
1936	Joined the St. John Ambulance Service at Northleach.
1937	Passed First Aid Examination. Did voluntary ambulance work.
1938	Volunteered for the Territorial Army Military Hospital Reserve.
1939	October 3rd — Called to the Cambridge Hospital Aldershot on declaration of war. October 4th — Transferred from TA to the Regular Army at Crookham Camp. October 7th — Joined the newly formed 2nd Light Field Ambulance. After kitting out, moved to Hertfordshire as part of 1st Armoured Division for intensive training in anti-gas procedure and evacuation of wounded.
1940	Joined the British Expeditionary Force in France. June 16th — Evacuated from Cherbourg following a rearguard battle on the Somme. Arrived back in England. Joined the 22nd Armoured Brigade. Moved into Surrey for defence of London, in case of enemy invasion.
1941	August 14th — Embarked from Avonmouth, and joined the 8th Army in Egypt and prepared for the winter offensive. November 9th — Moved up to wire and moved into Cyrenaica and on to Libya, having relieved Tobruk, and Benghazi. Several major tank battles *en route*. Halted at El-Agheila.
1942	Forced to retreat back into Egypt. October 23rd — Battle of El Alamein starts the final drive across the Western Desert. December — Field Ambulance withdrew from line for rest and refit, at Martuba, near Tobruk. December 23rd — Reported sick. Transported by ambulance to General Hospital Tobruk with infected hepatitis. December 24th — Christmas Eve spent on stretcher awaiting evacuation to Base Hospital. December 25th — Moved by Hospital Train to No.1 General Hospital at Kantara on the Suez Canal.
1943	January — Moved to R.A.M.C. Headquarters at Abyssia, near Cairo. Joined transport ship at Alexandria as medical attendant to gunners and crew. Sailed to Malta. Docked February 22nd. Joined staff of 90th General Hospital at M'tarfa.
1944	Completed finals in Medical and Surgical Examinations, also Hematology and Transfusion.

1945 June 30th — Married to Sister J. Palmer QAIMNS in Floriana, Malta.
August 14th — Tour of overseas duty completed. Return to England.
October 7th — Reported for duty at the Queen Victoria General Hospital, Netley, for duty until demobilization.

1946 July 21st — Discharged from the army.

1952 Joined the British Legion at Lyneham.

1953 Moved to Wantage, Berkshire.

1956 Helped form the Toc H branch in Wantage.

1957 Joined the Forgotten Allies with Sue Ryder, wife of Leonard Cheshire. Assisted in the adoption of two Polish families in Poland. Assisted with the Wantage Poppy Appeal. Became Scoutmaster for the L & A Scout Group.

1958 Organised campaign for the British Leprosy Association through Toc H.

1959 Became Parade Marshal for the district Remembrance Day Parades.

1960 Chairman Toc H. Formed Junior Toc H for amateur dramatics.

1961 Pilot to Toc H. Started Hospital Egg Week. Chairman to working parties of sixth formers of St. Mary's School and boys of The King Alfred Grammar School, in working for the elderly.

1962 Took over the care of the Soldiers Homes, Wantage.

1963 Royal British Legion Branch re-formed. Became Social Secretary and Representative of War Graves Commission.

1966 Organised Wantage Searchlight Tattoo. Chairman to Wantage Royal British Legion Pageant Committee.

1967 Chairman to Carnival Committee. Formed Wantage Silver Band.

1968 Chairman Royal British Legion Branch Wantage. Lost my wife in tragic road accident.

1969 Joined local branch of the Imperial Cancer Research Fund with P. Kay and family.

1971 Remarried to Elizabeth Kay of the ICR Fund.

1972 Chairman to Imperial Cancer Research Fund. Found and adopted L. Casbourne, ex-serviceman. He is now 92 years old. (1989). Awarded the Certificate of Appreciation from the Poppy Appeal with Poppy Pin, for services rendered. Royal British Legion Wantage Service Secretary.

1974 Awarded County Certificate for 21 years service to the RBL. Helped form The Festival of Remembrance Wantage.

1976 We formed the Sunshine Club for the Elderly at Marcham.

1982 Vice-President of Wantage Silver Band.
1985 President Wantage Royal British Legion. Trustee to Wantage Silver Band.
1986 Joined Federation of Old-Age Pensions.

Campaign and Service Medals

1939-1945 Star
The Africa Star and Bar
The Defence Medal
1939-1945 Medal
Territorial Army Volunteer Reserve (Hospital)

The Dunkirk Medal
The Ceux De La Somme Medal
Battle of Britain Com: Medal
The Royal British Legion Gold Badge for 34 years service to the cause.